CAN ADA EAST

MONTRÉAL
TORONTO
QUÉBEC

T0001651

Travel with Marco Polo
Insider Tips

MARCO POLO
TOP HIGHLIGHTS

CN TOWER ⭐
Toronto's famous landmark and, at 553m, one of the world's tallest towers.

📷 *Tip: With morning light over the city's towers – it's an enchanting sight*

➤ p. 43, Toronto

HOCKEY HALL OF FAME ⭐2
Pucks, hockey stars and the legendary Stanley Cup: Toronto's monument to Canada's most popular sport.

➤ p. 42, Toronto

NIAGARA FALLS ⭐3
The Iroquois used to call North America's biggest waterfalls the "thundering waters".

📷 *Tip: In the afternoon, a rainbow appears above the falls' steaming cauldron*

➤ p. 54, Ontario

NATIONAL GALLERY OF CANADA ⭐
From Inuit sculptures to photographs by Jeff Wall: Ottawa's treasure trove of Canadian art.

📷 *Tip: The giant spider at the entrance is a perfect selfie spot*

➤ p. 59, Ontario

POINTE-À-CALLIÈRE ⭐5
Follow in the tracks of the first settlers and fur traders deep below the metropolis of Montréal: urban archaeology can be fun.

➤ p. 73, Montréal

ROCHER PERCÉ ⭐
A distinctive monolith on the breathtaking coast of the Gaspé Peninsula, framed by wonderful colours in autumn.

➤ p. 93, Québec

HAUTE VILLE & BASSE VILLE ⭐

A picture-postcard sight: Québec's old town and walls date back over 400 years.

📷 *Tip: The best views of the city are from the ferry to Lévis*

➤ p. 85, Québec

PEGGY'S COVE ⭐

Canada's most beautiful fishing village, on the south coast of Nova Scotia, is now a magnet for tourists – and justifiably so!

📷 *Tip: Beware of high waves when taking photos on the rocks; another pretty spot is next to the tower*

➤ p.107, Atlantic Coast

CABOT TRAIL ⭐

300km of Atlantic panorama – high above the steep coastline of Cape Breton and in idyllic valleys (photo).

📷 *Tip: The best shots of coast and corniche are taken from the Skyline Trail*

➤ p. 109, Atlantic Coast

BOAT TRIP ON THE WESTERN BROOK POND ⭐

Newfoundland's inland fjords are more beautiful and remote than those in Norway, flanked by 600-m tall cliffs. Best explored by boat.

➤ p. 126, Newfoundland & Labrador

CONTENTS

NEWFOUNDLAND & LABRADOR

QUÉBEC

ONTARIO

MONTRÉAL

TORONTO

ATLANTIC COAST

CONTENTS

⏱ Plan your visit

C$–$$$ Price categories

(*) Premium rate phone number

🍴 Eating/drinking

🛍 Shopping

🍸 Going out

🏖 Top beaches

🏕 Rainy day activities

🐖 Budget activities

👯 Family activities

🚩 Classic experiences

(🗺 A2) Refers to the removable pull-out map
(🗺 a2) Refers to the inset street maps on the pull-out map
(0) Located off the map

BEST OF
CANADA
EAST

Lighthouse on the Île Verte in the St Lawrence River

BEST ☂ WHEN IT RAINS

ACTIVITIES TO BRIGHTEN YOUR DAY

MEET THE MUMMIES
Time flies in the *Royal Ontario Museum*. Despite an absence of royalty, you will encounter mummies, dinosaurs and a massive five-storey crystal.
➤ p. 45, Toronto

RIDE THE NIAGARA RIVER RAPIDS
It doesn't matter what the weather is like when you take an exciting high-powered *Whirlpool Jetboat Tour* through the towering rapids – you are going to get wet anyway!
➤ p. 54, Ontario

UNDERGROUND SHOPPING
Spend a rainy day in Montréal's *Ville Souterraine* without ever having to go outside. Almost 2,000 shops and restaurants offer lots of shopping fun (photo).
➤ p. 77, Montréal

MOURN THE TITANIC
When the heavens open up, a tour of artefacts from the *Titanic* seems very appropriate. Many reminders of the tragedy are preserved in the *Maritime Museum* and in several cemeteries.
➤ p. 105, Atlantic Coast

LIGHTHOUSE AHOY!
Bad weather also has its good side in *Peggy's Cove* and other harbour villages on Nova Scotia's south coast. The fog that typically swirls around the craggy harbours ensures particularly atmospheric photos.
➤ p. 107, Atlantic Coast

VIKINGS
Fog and drizzle are not uncommon in *L'Anse aux Meadows*. However, inside the recreated Viking huts you can get cosy on fur benches in front of the campfire, listening to "residents" recount ancient legends.
➤ p. 126, Newfoundland & Labrador

BEST ON A BUDGET

FOR SMALLER WALLETS

WINE FOR DINNER
Alcohol consumption is strictly regulated in Canada and is often expensive. Not in Québec, though, where you can buy wine and beer in grocery shops at surprisingly low prices. In Montréal, some restaurants allow you to bring your own wine *(apportez votre vin, BYOW)*.

SKYLINE PHOTOS
Sometimes, ferries are the cheapest way to get great photos: in Toronto, the *ferry to the Toronto Islands* offers wonderful views of the CN Tower and city skyline for just a few dollars. In Québec City, go to *Lévis* for a view of the city.
➤ p. 44, Toronto, p. 85 Québec

AVANT-GARDE TORONTO
Contemporary art can be enjoyed free of charge in Toronto: the *Power Plant Gallery* in the York Quay Centre on Toronto's waterfront curates four large-scale exhibitions every year, displaying design, photography and architecture by young artists.
➤ p. 44, Toronto

FREE MUSIC IN OTTAWA
During the summer the nation's capital celebrates a different festival almost every weekend – be it blues, jazz or Canada Day. These free concerts are funded by the *National Capital Commission*.
➤ p. 62, Ontario

DANCING DOLLS
This is not great art and the dolls don't actually dance, but the *Barbie Expo* (photo) in Montréal is still well worth a visit and is free of charge. On display are hundreds of Barbie dolls dressed in haute couture.
➤ p. 74, Montréal

BEST WITH CHILDREN

FUN FOR YOUNG & OLD

RV HOLIDAYS

Motor homes, or *RVs (recreational vehicles)* as they are known in Canada, are ideal for children: the vehicle provides a familiar environment, and the campsites are well looked after and spacious, often featuring playgrounds and pools. An adventure with campfires, fishing, canoeing and outdoor activities guarantees a great family holiday.

BE A PIONEER

Most Canadian museums offer programmes for children, but the *Canadian Children's Museum* is solely for kids: they can dress up, listen to fairy tales, climb aboard a Thai rickshaw… It's great fun all round.

➤ p. 60, Ontario

MOOSE WATCHING

Moose, beavers, bears and caribou can all be seen in the large forest enclosures of the *Zoo Sauvage de St-Félicien* (photo) by Lac Saint-Jean. *Daily in summer 9am–7pm | admission C$42, children C$30 | 2230, Blvd du Jardin | St-Félicien | zoosauvage. org |*

➤ p. 97, Québec

LIKE THE ADRIATIC SEA

The small resort village of *Cavendish* on the warm Gulf Stream coast off Prince Edward Island specialises in family holidays: with go-cart circuit, minigolf (or Black Magic Minigolf in the dark), children's zoo and waterslides.

➤ p. 113, Atlantic Coast

CHOCOLATE RAFTING

The torrents in the Bay of Fundy look like liquid chocolate. Exciting tidal rafting trips on the *Shubenacadie River* include mud slides and are great fun.

➤ p. 133, Discovery tours

AT THE BOTTOM OF THE FALLS

The truly impressive *Journey behind the Falls* brings you right to where you can feel – and peep behind – the vast curtain of water that is Niagara Falls.
➤ p. 54, Ontario

PADDLING ON LAKE OPEONGO

Lakes, moose, rocks and forest – in a word, solitude. This is the iconic image of Canada. A canoe tour in the *Algonquin Provincial Park* can make the dream come true (photo).
➤ p. 63, Ontario

ALONG THE RIVER OF THE WHALES

The St Lawrence estuary is home to more whale species than anywhere else on Earth. Around the *Mingan Archipelago* you can see blue, fin and humpback whales and take part in scientific observations.
➤ p. 99, Québec

FOLLOW THE CABOT TRAIL

Cape Breton Island offers the east coast's wildest, most beautiful and unspoilt panoramas. The 300-km *Cabot Trail* leads you past colourful fishing villages, rugged cliffs, lush valleys and scenic highlands – it's also ideal for a guided bike tour.
➤ p. 109, p.129, Atlantic Coast

DINNER WITH A VIEW

Perched on a cliff above the Bay of Fundy, *Cape d'Or Lighthouse* provides stunning views. You can watch one of the world's greatest tidal ranges here. The restaurant next door serves typical hearty chowder and fresh fish.
➤ p. 114, Atlantic Coast

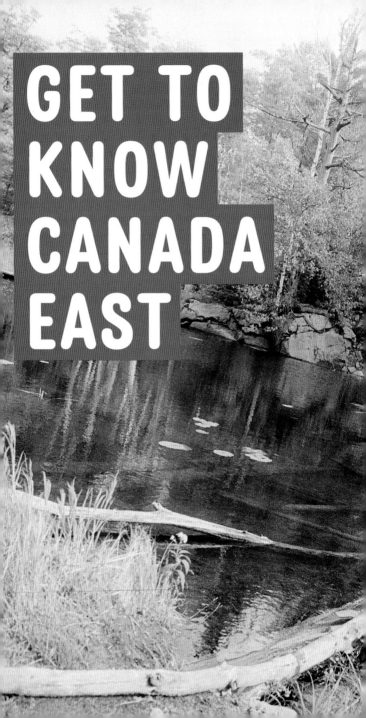

GET TO
KNOW
CANADA
EAST

DISCOVER CANADA EAST

Popular restaurants in Rue St-Vincent in Montréal's old town

Canada has become sexy, with cool cities, wild nature and great experiences on offer. And, with a magnificent system of national parks, excellent schools and innovative businesses, not to mention the polite and friendly people, you'll find it's a country well worth visiting.

A LOT TO DISCOVER

Although Niagara Falls and the wonderful autumnal woodland colours are at the top of Eastern Canada's list of attractions, there is plenty more to discover as well: one of the world's tallest towers in Toronto, trendy shops in Montréal and fine lobster restaurants on the Atlantic coast. Active visitors will love Canada's countryside too: a canoe tour through the quiet landscape of Algonquin Park; a trip to

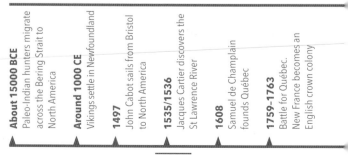

About 15000 BCE
Paleo-Indian hunters migrate across the Bering Strait to North America

Around 1000 CE
Vikings settle in Newfoundland

1497
John Cabot sails from Bristol to North America

1535/1536
Jacques Cartier discovers the St Lawrence River

1608
Samuel de Champlain founds Québec

1759–1763
Battle for Québec. New France becomes an English crown colony

the lighthouses of Nova Scotia; iceberg watching in Newfoundland; or a beach hike to one of the world's greatest tidal ranges.

MULTICULTURAL TOLERANCE

The English and the French were the predominant settler groups, but Germans, Italians and Ukrainians also settled here – and in recent decades immigration from Asia and the Caribbean has been on the increase. Canada favours a policy of cultural tolerance, meaning it is not a "melting pot of nations" like the United States, but a multicultural society. It is also committed to respect the rights of its indigenous people – the First Nations.

EVERYTHING IS BIGGER, LARGER & WILDER

Canada is the second largest country in the world with an area of 10 million km². From the Atlantic to the Pacific it measures over 5,500km and spans six time zones. The eastern half of the country is as big as Western Europe from Northern Norway to Gibraltar. Six times the size of the UK, the province of Québec (1.5 million km²) is the second largest province of Canada; the second smallest province, Ontario (1.1 million km²), is still four times as big as the UK. Yet only 37 million people live in Canada – of which two-thirds live in the eastern part. This means a population density of only four people per square kilometre.

While images of the Rocky Mountains in Canada's west are well known, the east impresses with its dramatic coastal landscape and the Great Lake districts. On the Atlantic coast, the steep cliffs of Labrador and Newfoundland rise from the

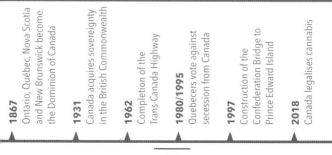

1867 Ontario, Québec, Nova Scotia and New Brunswick become the Dominion of Canada

1931 Canada acquires sovereignty in the British Commonwealth

1962 Completion of the Trans-Canada Highway

1980/1995 Quebecers vote against secession from Canada

1997 Construction of the Confederation Bridge to Prince Edward Island

2018 Canada legalises cannabis

sea. People live in fishing villages along the storm-tossed coast, where icebergs pass by in spring. Here, a car journey to the nearest town can take hours, if there's a road at all.

The climate is milder in the Atlantic provinces of Nova Scotia, Prince Edward Island and New Brunswick. Pretty harbour towns line the rocky coast. The densely forested mountains inland form part of the ancient Appalachians, over time eroded by glaciers to a soft low mountain range. Prince Edward Island, surrounded by potato fields, boasts Canada's warmest and most beautiful seashore.

ST LAWRENCE, GATEWAY TO CANADA

To the west the landscape joins the fertile St Lawrence lowlands, the former route of explorers and fur traders. In the provinces of Québec and Ontario lie the important metropolises and the economic heart of the industrial nation. Québec City, Montréal and Toronto – Canada's large cities – are strung like pearls along the St Lawrence river and Lake Ontario, with postmodern architecture and a colourful ethnic mixture, while the elegant capital, Ottawa, has numerous museums and manicured parks. And then, of course, there's thundering Niagara Falls, Eastern Canada's world-famous attraction.

North of the cities and the lush green farms of the lowlands starts the silent realm of the granite peaks and forests of the Canadian Shield. Shaped like a giant horseshoe, this region was created by glaciers, which formed Hudson Bay and thousands of lakes, untamed rivers and deep forests extending to the edge of the Arctic. The northern part of Ontario and Québec is popular with fishermen, canoeists and wilderness enthusiasts.

FROM KAYAKING TO MUSICALS

There are many adventures for you to experience, such as canoeing or kayaking in Algonquin Park, or hiking along the Cabot Trail in Nova Scotia. However, you don't have to push yourself to the limit all the time: a musical in Toronto, a chat in a Montréal bistro, a shopping spree in an elegant mall – these are also part of a trip to Canada. A tour through Ontario's lake landscape can give you a feeling of freedom and vastness. Then, by a campfire at sunset and with a moose grazing in the reed grass by a shallow lake, your stay becomes a dream holiday.

AT A GLANCE

25 MILLION
inhabitants of Ontario, Quebec and the Atlantic provinces

United Kingdom: 67 million

18.5kg
beef is eaten by the average Canadian every year
EU citizens: 10.5kg

8,200km^2
Lake Superior: largest lake (shared with the USA)

Lake Geneva: 580km^2

553m
CN Tower, Toronto:
highest tower in the Western hemisphere

HIGHEST PEAK:
Mont d'Iberville,
Mount Caubvick

1,652m

Ben Nevis 1,345m

COLDEST MONTH
JANUARY
-27°C
IN LABRADOR CITY

DAYS OF SNOWFALL
per year

93

in Saguenay, Québec

3,283,000km^2

area of Ontario, Québec and the Atlantic provinces combined
area of United Kingdom = 242,500km^2 (approx. 7.4%)

TORONTO

Largest Canadian city, with 6.4 million inhabitants

40 PER CENT
of Canadians have barbecues all year round

31 MILLION KG
OF LOBSTER IS CAUGHT IN
NOVA SCOTIA EACH YEAR

UNDERSTAND CANADA EAST

numerous animals including beaver, bear, lynx, deer, caribou and moose; there are even polar bears hunting seals in the decreasing pack ice in the far north of the Canadian Arctic.

BEAVERS & MAPLES

Glorious nature: Eastern Canada offers an amazing natural spectacle at the end of September: the so-called Indian summer. Maples and other trees glow in all shades of red and orange after the first night frosts. A 1,000-km-wide band of forest stretches across the country, with deciduous trees in the south and evergreens in the north, and populated by

FIRST NATIONS

The descendants of Canada's original inhabitants are today known as First Nations. Canadians now acknowledge the presence of the 617 tribes that lived in the country long before the settlers came and whose ancestors crossed the Bering Strait into North America during the ice age.

Over the course of millennia, independent cultural groups emerged, with semi-nomadic hunters living in the north and far east of Canada.

Inuit live in Labrador, Arctic Québec and Northern Ontario

However, the Iroquois and Hurons had a sedentary woodland culture and settled in the region around the St Lawrence river, cultivating corn, beans and tobacco. Further west lived the bison-hunting Plains tribes.

About a thousand years ago, the ancestors of today's Inuit settled in Alaska from the Canadian Arctic. They call themselves the *Inuit* (people) – not *Eskimo* as the term translates as "raw meat eater" and is considered derogatory.

The first decades of contact with the white settlers was not as traumatic for the Canadian natives as it was for their brothers in the United States. The fur traders were dependent on the Native Americans' support and had a limited impact on their way of life. However, diseases introduced by the Europeans decimated the tribes. Only with the settlement of the west during the 19th century were the First Nations forced into reservations. Today, with the improvement of health care, 700,000 Native Americans and 50,000 Inuit live in Canada.

PROTECTED FOREVER

The most famous of Canada's 47 national parks, including Banff and Jasper, are situated in Western Canada. But there are some beautiful, protected natural areas in the east, such as the lakes of La Mauricie, the cliffs of Forillon on the Gaspé Peninsula, the mountains of Cape Breton Island or the fjords of Gros Morne in Newfoundland. *parks canada.ca*

GOD SAVE THE QUEEN

Although she only performs the occasional ceremonial task, Queen Elizabeth II is Canada's head of state as the nation is a parliamentary democracy within the British Commonwealth. The Parliament in Ottawa is responsible for foreign policy, defence and finance. The ten Canadian provinces enjoy extensive autonomy, for example in education, culture, health care and the exploitation of natural resources.

GROUP OF SEVEN

During colonial times, the Canadian pioneers' main concern was to survive. It wasn't until the 20th century that Canada's artistic cultural scene emerged. The first – and best known – Canadian painting style was established in 1912 when young painters came together in Toronto as the "Group of Seven". Inspired by naturalist Tom Thomson, they developed a new expressive form of landscape painting. Today their paintings fetch prices of up to CAN$ 7 million.

GOING GREEN

In 2011, the then industry-focused government of Canada opted out of the Kyoto Protocol – a sad indictment of the founding country of Greenpeace, and a move motivated by financial reasons. However, many Canadians are environmentally aware with waste being separated and recycled, nature parks created and environmental organisations actively supported. Yet, compared to the rest of the world, the country is a big offender. Canadians

Mennonites prefer horsepower to cars

have always had plentiful resources – minerals, energy and water – and rethinking their ways takes time. It was not until 2015 that the country, under Prime Minister Justin Trudeau, signed the Paris Agreement.

JUSTIN

The Prime Minister of Canada is young and sexy. He portrays himself as being in touch with the people, lists boxing as his hobby and was a high school teacher prior to his election. Son of the former Prime Minister Pierre Trudeau – popular in the 1970s – Justin Trudeau has politics in his blood. Since his election in 2015, he has distinguished himself politically and, among other things, has brought women and minorities into the cabinet.

FURRY CREATURES

You will not meet grizzlies or polar bears on your trip through Eastern Canada. They live high in the Arctic and in the mountains of the west. However, there are black bears. Inquisitive and always hungry, they sniff through campsites at night, chase hikers from their blueberry territory or wander across the Trans-Canada Highway.

Always take your bear photos from a safe distance, store food in an air-tight container in your car at night and immediately wash your dishes after eating that steak. Black bears have an excellent sense of smell and good hearing, yet their eyesight is poor.

MENNONITES

In Mennonite country you will see horse-drawn carriages on the highway and farms without electricity: internet and telephone are taboo, as are cars and tractors! The deeply religious Mennonites are farmers who live according to old Christian ideals, and are sceptical about anything new. Their ancestors came to Canada in the 19th century from Germany and Switzerland, Russia and the United States. Here they found religious freedom.

As in times past, the women work in the kitchen and on the fields, while the men plough and harvest with horses, wagons and scythes. You will see them in the markets, talking in an archaic form of German. There are about 300,000 Mennonites in Canada today, some of them drive cars and are not as conservative as the Old Order Mennonites who live on their ancestral lands around Kitchener.

SWEET DELIGHTS

Canadians love their sweet donuts and coffee. The most popular place for both is the "Tim Hortons" chain, named after a famous ice hockey player. Try their French vanilla coffee and maple glazed donuts or dutchies with raisins. *Titbits* – the punched out donut holes – are delicious treats.

SIDER TIP
A sweet tip

"OUI" AND "YES"

Canada is a bilingual nation. From the milk cartons in the supermarkets to national park maps and the entry

TRUE OR FALSE?

ONLY IN FRENCH?

It isn't necessary to speak French to travel to Québec: in Montréal and Québec City both French and English are spoken. Hotel and restaurant staff are bilingual, as are sightseeing tours. The hinterland is another story: here some hardcore separatists don't like hearing English – at least if it comes from Canadian visitors; visitors from Europe get a much friendlier reception, and many Québecois who didn't understand *anglais* beforehand, suddenly turn out to be fluent English speakers.

LOBSTER EVERYWHERE

On the Atlantic coast, lobster is always on the menu. However, prices vary significantly, which is why "market price" is added. Each year, fishermen catch 90 million kilos of the delicious crustaceans off the Canadian coastline. Stocks are stable, as are fishing quotas. Prices rise and fall: in 2013 restaurants paid the fishermen C$3 for a pound while in 2019 it was C$9. When lobster is cheap, McDonalds serve a lobster roll… and rising prices see the McLobster disappearing from the menu.

forms at customs, the written word appears in both English and French. About 60 per cent of Canadians speak English and 30 per cent speak French as their mother tongue. However, the distribution is not even: in the Atlantic provinces, Ontario and the west, you will hear English almost exclusively; in Québec it is predominantly French.

Quebecers have guarded their culture over the centuries and are passionately French at heart, getting upset if Ottawa appears to marginalise their special status. Over the decades, the linguistic and cultural division has resulted in serious crises. Fifty years ago, the nationalist *Parti Québécois* demanded the total separation of Québec from Canada, leading to terrorist attacks by separatists. In 1980 and 1995, referendums on the issue were held. Both times, the majority of Québec's population decided against separation, albeit by small margins. And in recent elections, Justin Trudeau has benefited from his Montréal origins and French-Canadian support.

REDCOATS

Apart from the maple leaf, the Mounties – Royal Canadian Mounted Police – are probably Canada's most famous symbol. Their red parade uniforms are seen at official events and appear in many souvenir photos. However, the 15,000 strong RCMP are more than just colourful accessories: these highly trained police are responsible for all the rural regions and the places in Canada that cannot afford their own police force.

ZAMBONI

No other sport embodies the Canadian soul as well as ice hockey: during

The colourful Royal Canadian Mountain Police

Canadians love donuts – even as picture frames

Hockey Night, the whole nation sits spellbound in front of the television. Children as young as five years learn to ice skate and know what a *Zamboni* is – a machine that resurfaces the ice rink. The professional players are national heroes. Everybody knows them and the names of legendary teams, such as the *Canadiens de Montréal* or the Toronto Maple Leafs.

However, the official national sport is lacrosse, a fast ball game with First Nation origins. Every major city has its team and the sport has become fashionable once again.

NATURAL RESOURCES

Canada is immensely rich in natural resources: the ancient rock of the Canadian Shield, in northern Ontario, Québec and Labrador, holds large deposits of iron, zinc, nickel and gold. The rivers of Québec provide virtually unlimited energy, and Newfoundland has oil. But Canada is trying to move away from its traditional role as raw material supplier to the rest of the world. Today, industrial production centred in southern Ontario around Toronto, Hamilton and Windsor counts for three-quarters of Canada's GDP. Nevertheless, for many Canadians the export of natural resources seems like a sell-out of the country. Electricity from the huge hydroelectric power stations in Québec is sold to the United States at low prices, while cheap wood from Ontario ends up as newspapers on breakfast tables all over the world.

EATING
SHOPPING
SPORT

Shopping mall in Montréal

EATING & DRINKING

There is no Canadian national dish: the country is simply too big and the population is too diverse. Immigrant groups have come from all over the world and it is this multicultural diversity that is the charm of Eastern Canada's cuisine.

FROM AROUND THE WORLD

In Toronto you can eat excellent Chinese, Ukrainian and Polish food. In Montréal you can enjoy French, Portuguese or Jewish kosher food. And, of course, there are the dishes that Canada is famous for: steaks from Alberta (with baked potatoes and corn on the cob with butter), lobster from the Atlantic coast and all kinds of fresh salmon.

Further inland, in Ontario, the Niagara Peninsula with its mild climate produces fresh vegetables, delicious wine and excellent fruit.

FRENCH HERITAGE

The cuisine of Québec deserves a chapter of its own. For centuries the province has been the culinary core of Canada. Immigrants from Normandy and Brittany, who were mostly fishermen and farmers, brought their recipes to the New World. Due to a lack of ingredients, they often had to modify their recipes. Instead of pork, beef or chicken, they used moose, deer, wild turkey or goose. From the First Nations, they learned how to prepare corn and pumpkin, and instead of using sugar they sweetened their food with vitamin-rich maple syrup, protecting themselves from scurvy in late winter.

FINE SEAFOOD

Along the Atlantic coast, lobster, fish and shellfish are on the menu. The lobster – which grows slowly in the cold Atlantic – is considered the best in

Distillery Historic District in Toronto (left) and smoked salmon bagel (right)

the world. On Prince Edward Island massive lobster suppers are served in community and church halls. Pubs and sometimes McDonald's in small harbour towns serve lobster rolls. The large scallops are equally good. Scottish immigrants brought the recipe for *Solomon Gundy* – delicious, marinated herring – to Nova Scotia. However, some traditional recipes from Newfoundland take a bit of getting used to – for example fried cod tongues. Better known, and always good and fresh, are the calamari which are fished off the coast of Newfoundland. From the lakes in the hinterland, pike, whitefish and perch are often served together with wild rice, which the Native Americans harvest from the northern lakes.

WHAT TO EAT & WHEN?

Coffee shops are your best bet for breakfast. Sometimes they are part of the hotel or are close to motels. You can either enjoy a small continental breakfast (juice, coffee, toast with marmalade) or order a large American breakfast with eggs, bacon and fried potatoes. Coffee is topped up free of charge but it is often really weak; you can order a cappuccino or latte instead. You will only find stronger brewed Americano coffee in Québec.

For lunch, between noon and 2pm, Canadians eat smaller cheaper dishes, usually a simple Caesar salad or soup and sandwich. In rural regions, dinner is served early, between 5.30pm and 7pm; in the larger cities it's between 7pm and 10pm. In most restaurants you will need to wait to be shown to your table.

Be aware that the prices shown on the menu do not include tax, which differs from province to province and only appears on the bill. The tip is not usually included; if you are happy

Lobster is a classic dish in the Atlantic provinces

the fashionable microbreweries with adjoining pub which often serve great ales and even wheat beer. Wine is served in most restaurants, while in small un-licensed restaurants in

INSIDER TIP
Bring your own wine

Québec you can bring your own. Good wines from California or France are often on the menu, but do try the local wine from Nova Scotia or the Niagara Peninsula. If you like stronger drinks, you can rely on the excellent Canadian whiskey, which is either served on the rocks or – like rum or gin – in mixed drinks.

with the service, a 15–18% tip is the norm. Just leave it on the table or add it to your credit card bill.

DRINKS

If there is a national drink in Canada, then it is *beer* – aromatic and very palatable, especially when compared to the watery American beer. Everywhere in the country you will find Molson Canadian or Labatt's Blue, while speciality beers such as Moosehead are served only in some regions. Popular meeting points are

KISS THE FISH

A popular tradition of Newfoundland is the *screech-in*. If it is your first time on the island, you will hardly be able to escape it. Be it in private or in a bar, the ritual is always the same: the new-comer has to put on the islanders' typical waterproof hat, kiss a freshly caught cod (or any other large fish) and drink a glass of pure high-proof Newfoundland rum. Then you become an honorary Newfoundlander.

Crown Royal is a popular Canadian whiskey brand

Today's Specials

Starters / Snacks

CLAM CHOWDER

MALPEQUE OYSTERS
Oysters from Malpeque Bay on Prince Edward Island

SOUPE AUX POIS
Hearty pea soup from Québec

POUTINE
French fries with Cheddar cheese and gravy

Main courses

SEARED SALMON WITH ROOT VEGETABLES

LOBSTER WITH DRAWN BUTTER AND CORN ON THE COB

RIBEYE WITH GARLIC MASHED POTATOES

LOBSTER MAC AND CHEESE

TOURTIÈRE
Meat pie from Québec with minced pork, beef and spices

Desserts

TARTE AUX BLEUETS A LA MODE
Québec blueberry tart with a scoop of ice cream

BEAVERTAILS
Shortbread dusted with cinnamon and sugar

MAPLE CRÈME BRÛLÉE
Crème brûlée with maple syrup

PUMPKIN PIE WITH WHIPPED CREAM

Drinks

CAESAR
Spicy drink made with vodka and clamato (clam and tomato) juice

IPA BEER

CARIBOU
Red wine punch, a winter speciality from Québec

SHOPPING

Prices are usually similar to those in Europe. Casual and sportswear, vitamin pills and some food specialities are cheaper in Canada than in many other countries, and you can find real bargains at the sales.

There is plenty of choice in the cities, but in the hinterland your shopping options decrease dramatically. Make sure you fully stock your camper van before embarking on a long cross-country trip.

FOOD & DRINK

The most famous souvenir from Canada is maple syrup. The thickened sap from maple trees usually comes from the deciduous forests of Québec and is an essential part of a hearty pancake breakfast in Canada. Its crystallised sugar is used in chocolates and biscuits. Tasty souvenirs also include wine from the Niagara Peninsula (ice wine in particular), blueberry jelly from Lac St-Jean, lobster or smoked salmon from the Atlantic or sausages from the Mennonites in Kitchener.

ARTS & CRAFTS

Canadians love arts and crafts and most places have craft fairs in summer, offering turned wooden bowls, glass art, quirky ceramics or watercolour paintings. The crafts shops in the Atlantic provinces are excellent, selling sailing accessories for yachties, knitted pullovers from Newfoundland and CDs of Irish-Celtic immigrant music, still played by modern artists such as Ashley MacIsaac or the tap dance group Leahy.

INSIDER TIP
Dance along to fiddle music

FIRST NATION ART

Following ancient traditions, the Algonquin, Iroquois and Ojibwa tribes

Maple syrup (left), Ville Souterraine in Montréal (right)

produce baskets decorated with porcupine quills, beaded leather jackets and moccasins from moose leather. Typical of the region are small boxes and baskets from moulded birch bark. The Arctic Inuit are famous for their soapstone sculptures, which are also sold in galleries in Montréal, Toronto and Ottawa (from C$300). More affordable are art prints, like the ones produced by the Inuit in Cape Dorset or Pangnirtung.

MALLS & MARKETS

Shopping malls, departments stores and boutiques are everywhere in major cities. In Toronto, the *Eaton Centre* is popular, while in Montréal the *Rue Ste-Catherine* is the main shopping street. Some places have vast shopping complexes to escape the bitterly cold winters – such as the *Ville*

INSIDER TIP
Underground shopping

Souterraine in Montréal with more than 30km of underground passages connecting 2,000 shops.

Some of the old harbour districts have been renovated recently, such as the *Historic Properties* area in Halifax or Toronto's chic *Waterfront* shopping district around Queens Quay. In Toronto, visitors flock to trendy *West Queen Street* while *Boulevard St-Laurent* is popular in Montréal.

Glass blowing, Halifax

SPORT & ACTIVITIES

Whether it be a traditional round of golf or a game of tennis, or something more modish such as kitesurfing, Canadians are enthusiastic about sport. Since pioneer times, the outdoor life has been in their blood. And nature offers them ideal conditions and fabulous scenery for outdoor activities, often within easy reach of the cities. In addition, every major hotel and resort has its own fitness centre and activity desk where you can book tee-off times for the on-site golf course and obtain information about activities in the area.

Many rental shops in parks and cities hire canoes, bicycles and other sporting equipment – and can also provide tips and maps. Organised day tours can be booked on the spot or at short notice, while cycling, diving or kayaking excursions lasting several days are best booked in advance.

CANOEING, RAFTING & KAYAKING

Trekking through the wilderness, just like the Native Americans and trappers once did, is one of Canada's most beautiful experiences. Canoes can be rented (hourly or daily) at many lodges and outfitters – and there are scenic lakes everywhere. Areas of true wilderness, where you can follow in the footsteps of fur traders, can be found in northern Ontario and in national parks such as Mauricie or Kejimkujik. Sea kayaking is popular in sheltered ocean bays (ontarioparks. com/paddling and aventurequebec. ca/en/canoeing).

Good rafting trips are offered on the Ottawa River at Beachburg, west of Ottawa, by Wilderness Tours (tel. 888 7 23 86 69 | wildernesstours.com). Canoe rental and beautiful multi-day canoe trips with tent or cabin accommodation are offered in the west of

Sea kayaking at Rocher Percé

Algonquin Park by *Voyageur Quest Lodge (Round Lake, Algonquin Park | tel. 416 4 86 36 05 | voyageurquest.com).*

CYCLING

There are good routes for multi-day trips on Cape Breton Island, Prince Edward Island (PEI), the country roads in southern Ontario around Kitchener and along the St Lawrence downstream from Québec City. Canada has bicycle rental companies in most cities *(prices: C$15–35 per day, C$80–200 per week).*

MacQueen's (430 Queen St. | Charlottetown | tel. 902 3 68 24 53 | macqueens.com) has bicycles for hire and organises trips on PEI Bicycle hire for trips on the waterfront in Toronto and to the Toronto Islands are offered by *Wheel Excitement (249 Queens Quay W | behind the Radisson Admiral Hotel | tel. 416 2 60 90 00 | wheel excitement.ca).*

On the ▰ *Cabot Trail* in Nova Scotia, *Cabot Trail Adventures (299 Shore Rd | South Harbour | tel. 902 3 83 25 52 | cabottrailoutdooradventures.com)* offer guided tours and bicycle and kayak hire.

DIVING

You wouldn't think Canada had much to offer in the way of underwater adventure. However, its crystal-clear waters provide perfect diving conditions, and you can look for lobsters in the rock crevices and explore shipwrecks. The coast of *Nova Scotia* (Sable Island was formerly known as the graveyard of the Atlantic) and the *Bruce Peninsula* in Lake Huron are excellent diving sites. But you will need to have some experience and bring a wetsuit (or dry suit) for the icy Atlantic waters.

Individual diving tours off the south coast of Nova Scotia and to the icebergs in Labrador can be booked at *Vipi Lodge (West Arichat, NS | tel. 902*

5 63 15 07 | vipi lodge.com). One-day or multi-day dive excursions to the wrecks of whaling ships off the coast of Newfoundland and whale watching are offered by *Ocean Quest (17 Stanley's Lane | Conception Bay South | tel. 709 8 34 72 34 | oceanquestadventures. com)* near St John's.

For diver information about the Bruce Peninsula and surrounding area visit the *Tobermory Visitors Guide (tobermory.com).*

FISHING

Fishing in the many lakes and rivers is straightforward but you need a permit. Depending on the province and permit period, fishing licences (available at sport shops and lodges) cost C$45–70 for a week's holiday fishing, or C$160 for the coveted Atlantic salmon sport fishing.

National parks' licences are available at visitor centres. In the deserted north of the provinces, fishing enthusiasts will find ideal spots on numerous lakes – home to perch, whiting and gutsy pike.

Halley's Camps – offering a selection of isolated fly-in lodges and wilderness camps in the north-west of Ontario – are an ideal choice for passionate anglers *(Minaki | tel. 807 2 24 65 31 | halleyscamps.com).* Slightly less remote and accessible by

Fishing on the remote lakes of Ontario

Enjoy Canada's unspoilt Atlantic coast on a hack along the shoreline

car is *Tornado's Resort (Port Loring | tel. 705 7 57 30 03 | tornadosresorts. com)*: the actual fishing camps can only be reached by seaplane or boat.

HIKING

The largest selection of trails – signposted and well maintained – can be found in the national and provincial parks. The wardens in the visitor centres are happy to provide information about the best trails. Good networks are offered, e.g. on *Cape Breton Highlands*, the *Gaspé Peninsula* and *Bruce Peninsula*. Outside of the parks, hiking is often difficult – in Canada wilderness really does mean wilderness. The *Trans-Canada Trail*, the world's longest trail, crosses all provinces from Newfoundland to the Pacific coast . It's possible to hike individual legs of this route *(tctrail.ca)*.

INSIDER TIP
Crossing Canada

HORSE RIDING

The large ranches are mainly in the west of Canada, but you can also go riding in the countryside in the east. Watch out for signs by trail riding outfitters who advertise on the highways. You don't need to be an experienced rider to give it a go as they use wide Western saddles and the good-natured horses walk obediently in line.

WINTER FUN

Although the few ski slopes cannot compare to the powder snow of the Rockies, you can still take part in snowshoe hiking, sledding, ice fishing and snowmobiling at various winter sport centres. Recommended is *Deerhurst Resort (1235 Deerhurst Dr. | Huntsville | tel. 705 7 89 64 11 | deerhurstresort.com)*, a winter lodge west of the Algonquin Provincial Park.

REGIONAL OVERVIEW

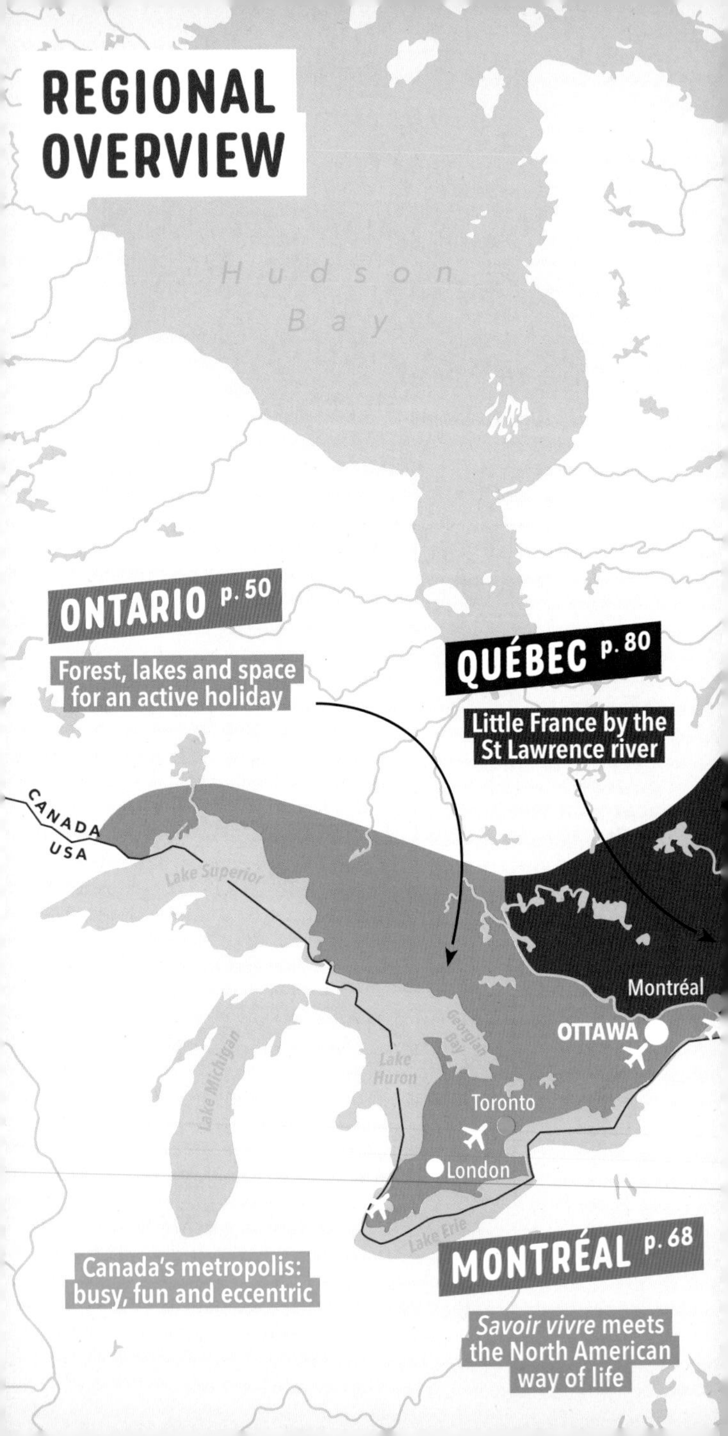

Hudson Bay

ONTARIO p. 50

Forest, lakes and space
for an active holiday

QUÉBEC p. 80

Little France by the
St Lawrence river

CANADA
USA

Lake Superior

Lake Michigan

Georgian Bay

Lake Huron

Montréal

OTTAWA

Toronto

London

Lake Erie

MONTRÉAL p. 68

Canada's metropolis:
busy, fun and eccentric

Savoir vivre meets
the North American
way of life

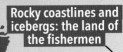

**NEWFOUNDLAND &
LABRADOR** p. 118

Rocky coastlines and
icebergs: the land of
the fishermen

Labrador

Sea

St John's

St Lawrence River

Gulf of
St. Lawrence

Québec

Fredericton

Halifax

ATLANTIC COAST p.100

Coves, cliffs and the
open sea

Gulf of
Maine

ATLANTIC

OCEAN

200 km
124.3 mi

TORONTO

Toronto was saved by its immigrants. Seventy years ago, the capital of Ontario was a sleepy provincial city – white, Anglo-Saxon and Protestant.

A wave of immigrants after World War II swelled the population to almost 6.2 million and transformed Toronto into a modern and lively global city *(seetorontonow.com)*. Today, the sprawling city on Lake Ontario is the engine of the country's economy. The centre is filled with the mirrored glass towers of high finance companies. Around it,

View of Toronto and the Gooderham Building

a colourful mosaic of ethnic neighbourhoods is evident in the hustle and bustle of Chinatown, Portuguese markets, Greek tavernas and Caribbean clubs.

The city is also a meeting place of young avant-garde and creative people who are tapping into Toronto's multicultural energy. The national ballet and opera have their home here. Toronto is worthy of its Native American name, which means "gathering place".

TORONTO

McMichael Canadian Art Collection ★

Drake Commissary

Mars

MARCO POLO HIGHLIGHTS

★ **HOCKEY HALL OF FAME**
The ultimate attraction for ice hockey
fans. Exhibits include the Stanley Cup
➤ p. 42

★ **CN TOWER**
Fantastic view from one of the world's
tallest towers plus a revolving
restaurant near the top ➤ p. 43

★ **QUEEN STREET WEST**
The city's most popular and fashionable
street: pubs, eccentric shops and tattoo
studios ➤ p. 44

★ **MUSEUM OF CONTEMPORARY
CANADIAN ART (MOCCA)**
Stage for the avant-garde, hidden away
in the industrial quarter ➤ p. 44

★ **ROYAL ONTARIO MUSEUM**
Spectacular architecture by Daniel
Libeskind ➤ p. 45

★ **EATON CENTRE**
Ideal for a spending spree: Toronto's
massive shopping centre has 350 shops
➤ p. 47

★ **ST LAWRENCE MARKET**
Market hustle and bustle with a
fabulously varied selection ➤ p. 48

★ **MCMICHAEL CANADIAN ART
COLLECTION**
The biggest collection of Canadian art
➤ p. 49

15 Royal Ontario Museum ★

18 Aga Khan Museum

Pantheon
Riverdale Farm
Toronto Zoo **19**

The Beaches **17**

The Beaches

Bloor Street West

Bata Shoe Museum

Queen's Park

St. George Street

Bay Street

Yonge Street

Church Street

Jarvis Street

Sherbourne Street

Parliament Street

Carlton Street

Sherbourne Street

Dundas Street East

College Street

Beverley Street

University Av.

Elm Street

Spadina Avenue

3 Art Gallery of Ontario

4 China-town

Eaton Centre ★

Shuter Street

Queen Street East

Queen Street West ★

12 **2** Bay Street

1 Nathan Phillips Square

Path

King Street East

Front Street East

Distillery Historic District **16**

Peter Pan Bistro

The Keg

St Lawrence Market ★

Adelaide Street West

Canoe

5 Hockey Hall of Fame ★

Gardiner Expy

Kit Kat

Rodney's Oyster House

Front Street West

Yonge Street

Queens Quay East

CN Tower ★ **6** **7** Ripley's Aquarium

8 Harbourfront

10 Toronto Music Garden

Inner Harbour

Airfield

Lakeshore Avenue

9 Toronto Islands

Hanlan Beach

Chelsea Beach

Lakeshore Avenue

20 km
12.43 mi

TORONTO

SIGHTSEEING

The 🐷 *Citypass* coupon ticket allows you to visit five of the city's top attractions for C$64 (30% discount), including the *CN Tower*, *Ripley's Aquarium* and the *Royal Ontario Museum*.

1 NATHAN PHILLIPS SQUARE

This urban plaza is the heart of Toronto. The *New City Hall,* designed in 1965 by the Finnish architect Viljo Revell, has a forecourt with fountains. On the east side is the Old Town Hall from 1899 and the chic Eaton Centre. Queen Street West runs along the south of the square, while Yonge Street, with numerous shops and restaurants, runs behind the Eaton Centre. ⚏ *h3*

2 BAY STREET

On Canada's "Wall Street", between Queen and Front streets, the *Royal Bank* shows off its wealth: more than 2,500 ounces of gold have been melted into the mirrored windows of its towers.

The financial district's most conspicuous building is *Brookfield Place*. Its avant-garde *Galleria*, designed by Spanish architect Santiago Calatrava, is reminiscent of the light-filled interior of a Gothic cathedral. ⚏ *g–j 1–4*

3 ART GALLERY OF ONTARIO

This, one of the best art museums in Canada, has an extension by star

WHERE TO START?

The central starting point is **City Hall** *(⚏ h3).* From there it is not far west to the Art Gallery of Ontario, Chinatown, the adjacent Kensington Market quarter and vibrant and colour-ful Queen Street West. If you feel like some serious shopping, head east to the Eaton Centre where you will also find a large car park close to the Queen and Osgoode subway stations.

architect Frank Gehry. The collection of around 900 works in the *Henry Moore Sculpture Centre* is a highlight. The private collections include works by old masters as well as European impressionists and surrealists. There are Inuit prints and works by contemporary Canadian artists as well as major touring exhibitions. *Tue, Thu 10.30am–5pm, Wed, Fri 10.30am–9pm, Sat/Sun 10.30am–5.30pm | admission C$19.50 | 317 Dundas St W | ago.ca |* ⚏ *g3*

4 CHINATOWN

Around the intersection of Dundas Street and Spadina Avenue, only a stone's throw from the Art Gallery of Ontario, you will find the best Chinese, Thai and Vietnamese restaurants and exotic shops. ⚏ *g3*

5 HOCKEY HALL OF FAME ★

Showcasing everything related to the sport, there are exhibitions about the ice legend Wayne Gretzky, jerseys from all over the world, details on Canada's Olympic triumphs and interactive exhibitions. Also on show is the legendary *Stanley Cup*, Canada's most important trophy. *Mon–Sat 9.30am–6pm, Sun 10am–6pm | admission C$20 | Brookfield Place | 30 Yonge St | hhof.com | ⏱ 1 hr | ▥ j3*

6 CN TOWER ★ 🐾

Built in 1975, the CN Tower remained the highest free-standing tower in the world for 30 years; the view over Toronto and 100km of the surrounding area is still terrific. The top observation deck (indoors) is 447m high, while the open-air terrace with glass floor is at 342m. One floor up you can enjoy the view from the "360" revolving restaurant.

Guaranteed to provide a unique experience and a real test of courage is the *EdgeWalk*: at a height of 356m you can free-walk around the tower on a broad ledge – with safety rope attached of course. There is also a flight simulator at the foot of the tower. *301 Front St W | daily 9am–10.30pm | admission C$38, EdgeWalk C$195 | cntower.ca | ▥ h4*

INSIDER TIP
Balancing act for the brave

Next to the CN Tower is the *Rogers Centre*, home stadium of the baseball team Blue Jays; it can seat 60,000 spectators and the 11,000-ton roof

In winter, the artificial lake in Nathan Phillips Square becomes an ice rink

can open and close in just 20 minutes *(daily guided tours | admission C$16 | 1 Blue Jays Way | tel. 416 3 41 27 70)*. The Maple Leafs hockey team is based two streets to the east in the *Scotiabank Arena*.

7 RIPLEY'S AQUARIUM 🐵
You'll find sharks, rays and jellyfish: 450 species and a total of 16,000 marine animals in a giant exhibition, including a nearly 100m-long glass tunnel through the shark tank. *Daily 9am–11pm | admission C$37, children C$25 | 288 Bremner Blvd | ripleyaquariums.com | ⏱ 2 hrs | ⊞ h4*

8 HARBOURFRONT
After many years of neglect, Toronto's waterfront piers along Lake Ontario have been given a new lease of life with marinas, shopping complexes and new glass apartment towers.

Along Queens Quay boats depart for harbour cruises and cafés invite you to linger. In the *York Quay Centre* young artists show their talent in workshops and galleries and at the leading 🐷 *Power Plant Contemporary Art Gallery*. It's no wonder half of Toronto seems to be strolling between *Queens Quay Terminal* and *Pier 4* at weekends. *harbourfrontcentre.com | ⊞ h–j 4–5*

9 TORONTO ISLANDS
The small island group around 3km from the harbour front on Lake Ontario offers a fantastic view of Toronto's skyline. There are also parks, a small amusement park for kids, cafés, cycling paths (bicycles for hire) and

beaches such as the child-friendly 🐵 🐵 *Chelsea Beach* and 🐵 *Hanlan Beach*, which has a nudist section.

Ferry service (13 mins) from the beginning of Bay St 🐷 C$8 | toronto island.com | ⊞ E13

10 TORONTO MUSIC GARDEN
In 1999 the famous cellist Yo-Yo Ma collaborated with a landscape designer to establish this unique waterfront garden, inspired by Bach's Cello Suite No. 1 in G Major. Frequent concerts are programmed in summer. 🐷 *Admission free | 475 Queens Quay W, between Bathurst St and Spadina St | ⊞ g–h5*

11 FORT YORK
In this fort, built in 1793, soldiers don original uniforms and illustrate the way of life in the former garrison. *In summer daily 10am–5pm, otherwise 10am–4pm, weekends until 5pm | admission C$14 | 250 Fort York Blvd | ⊞ g5*

12 QUEEN STREET WEST ⭐
Buzzing at weekends, Queen Street west of City Hall is lined with chic boutiques, fashionable restaurants and bars. Beyond Spadina Avenue are numerous art galleries, second-hand shops and design ateliers. Don't miss the crazy murals in the side streets around *Graffiti Alley (Rush Lane)*. ⊞ g3

13 MUSEUM OF CONTEMPORARY CANADIAN ART (MOCCA) ⭐
In 2018 MOCCA moved to a 5,000-m2 historic industrial building which was

American designer Jeremy Scott is known for pushing the limits of design and for finding inspiration in many things from stuffed animals to computer keyboards. For his Totem collection, Scott turned to the traditional art of the West Coast First Nations peoples. Based on traditional totem pole designs, the sneakers have not been without criticism concerning cultural misappropriation.

Jeremy Scott for Adidas Totem, 2013

Collection of the Bata Shoe Museum

Not just winged shoes – the Bata Shoe Museum has 12,000 exhibits

Toronto's tallest when constructed in 1919. It is in the fashionable quarter of Lower Junction, west of the city, where a few avant-garde galleries and new restaurants have opened in former factories and car repair shops. *Wed–Mon 10am–5pm, Fri until 9pm | admission C$10 | 158 Sterling Rd | museumofcontemporaryart.ca | ⏱ 1 hr | ▥ E13*

14 BATA SHOE MUSEUM

A shoe box-shaped building contains the only shoe museum in North America. You can see every type of footwear from ancient Egyptian sandals to Elton John's show boots, Elvis's blue suede shoes and Manolo Blahnik creations from *Sex in the City*. *Mon–Sat 10am–5pm,*

INSIDER TIP
Blue suede shoes – Elvis lives on

Sun noon–5pm, Thu until 8pm | admission C$14 | 327 Bloor St W | batashoemuseum.ca | ▥ E13

15 ROYAL ONTARIO MUSEUM ★ ☂ ⚲

In 2007, Canada's largest museum received a noteworthy architectural accent: Daniel Libeskind designed the extension that rises up like a sparkling crystal. Inside is a collection of dinosaur skeletons, Egyptian mummies, Chinese temple art and Native American embroidery. There are also temporary exhibitions. Opposite is the *George R Gardiner Museum of Ceramic Art* with an excellent collection of majolica and Meissen porcelain. *Daily 10am–5.30pm, Fri 10am–8.30pm | admission C$20 | 100 Queen's Park | rom.on.ca | ⏱ 3 hrs | ▥ g1*

16 DISTILLERY HISTORIC DISTRICT

Today the old distillery east of the city centre is a monument to industrial history. Coffee shops, galleries and al fresco bars now occupy the old brick buildings. The photos, caps and team uniforms in the *Sport Gallery* are worth seeing. Frequent festivals are programmed on summer weekends. *55 Mill St | thedistillerydistrict.com | E13*

17 THE BEACHES

This young, laid-back beach and residential district has a promenade on the lake shore. You can find good boutiques and restaurants in *Queen Street East*. On summer weekends the *✻* sea at the foot of *Beaches Park* invites you to swim. *Tram 501 | E13*

18 AGA KHAN MUSEUM

The legacy of the Aga Khan who has long-standing connections with Canada: the museum, housed in a super-modern building that was created in 2014 by Japanese architect Fumihiko Maki, is home to a unique collection of Islamic art. *Tue–Sun 10am–6pm, Wed untill 8pm | admission C$20 | 77 Wynford Dr. | agakhanmuseum.org | E13*

INSIDER TIP
For lovers of architecture

19 TORONTO ZOO 🐵

What about a ride on a camel or on the Zoomobile across the 7-km² grounds with more than 5,000 animals? Small children can enjoy the *Discovery Zone* with children's zoo, water park and polar bear enclosure. *Daily in summer 9am–7pm, otherwise 9.30am–4.30pm | admission C$29, children C$19 | Hwy 401 | Meadowvale Rd | torontozoo.com | ⏱ 3 hrs | E13*

EATING & DRINKING

CANOE

Elegant and expensive: Canadian haute cuisine overlooking the skyscrapers from the 54th floor of the TD Bank. Slightly cheaper lunch menu. *66 Wellington St W | tel. 416 3 64 00 54 | C$$$ | E13*

DRAKE COMMISSARY

The barstools in this cool restaurant in the creative Junction Triangle quarter only have one armrest – to promote interaction! Great food and drinks and its own bakery. *128 Sterling Rd | tel. 416 4 23 29 22 | C$-$$ | E13*

THE KEG

Chic steak restaurant serving prime meat from Alberta, with a large bar where young business people hang out after work. *165 York St | tel. 416 7 03 17 73 | C$$-$$$ | h3*

KIT KAT

Quirky Italian restaurant with an attractive courtyard. *297 King St W | tel. 416 9 77 44 61 | C$$ | h3–4*

MARS

Bacon and eggs, *griddle cakes*, hamburgers: an iconic diner that has been offering the best and cheapest *coffee shop food* in the city since 1951.

Most dishes cost under C$10. All-day breakfast. *432 College St | tel. 921 63 32 | C$ | ⏷ E13*

PANTHEON

Souvlaki and moussaka in the middle of the Greek district, which is also popular for a stroll at night. *407 Danforth Ave | tel. 416 7 78 19 29 | C$ | ⏷ E13*

PETER PAN BISTRO

Cosy small restaurant in a fashionable quarter with a limited but excellent menu. *373 Queen St W | tel. 416 7 92 38 38 | C$-$$ | ⏷ H3*

RODNEY'S OYSTER HOUSE

Rustic vaulted cellar with a fish market and lively restaurant. Speciality: oysters and lobster. Terrace above in the courtyard. *469 King St W | tel. 416 3 63 81 05 | C$$ | ⏷ g4*

SHOPPING

Bloor, *Yonge* and *Queen Street* are the main shopping streets. Elegant shops can be found in *Yorkville* while the multicultural *Kensington Market* area *(Kensington Ave, north of Dundas St)* has second-hand clothes shops, avant-garde galleries and small ethnic restaurants.

EATON CENTRE ★

For a stunning shopping experience, this three-storey mall has 250 shops, two department stores and a snow goose sculpture by Michael Snow. *Yonge St, between Dundas St and Queen St | torontoeatoncentre.com | ⏷ h2*

PATH ☂

The perfect place to shop in bad weather: a 30-km network of

A roof like folded paper and extraordinary Islamic art: Aga Khan Museum

ECLECTIC

Avant-garde hotel with night club, rooftop cinema and sushi bar: *The Drake (19 rooms | 1150 Queen St W | tel. 416 5 31 50 42 | thedrakehotel.ca | C$$ | ⊞ E13)*.

MARVELLOUS VIEWS

Almost all 400 chic rooms of the new *Hotel X (111 Princess Blvd | tel. 647 9 43 93 00 | hotelxtoronto.ca | C$$-$$$ | ⊞ E13)* offer fabulous views of Lake Ontario and the city's skyline. There's a pool and rooftop bar. It makes an ideal city break for motorhome holidaymakers who can use the big car parks next door.

Gourmet heaven in St Lawrence Market

pedestrian tunnels, shopping arcades and malls that connect many of the larger buildings in the city centre. *torontopath.com* ⊞ *h–j3*

ST LAWRENCE MARKET ★

Since 1803 there has been a market here every Saturday. The butchers, fishmongers and bakeries in the southern part of the building are also open on weekdays – and bacon on a bun in the *Carousel Bakery* is a tradition. *Front St/Jarvis St | stlawrencemarket.com | ⊞ j3*

ENTERTAINMENT

What's on Tonight sells tickets for concerts, musicals and theatres on the day via an app *(whatsontonight.ca)* and 🐷 leftover tickets over the following weeks at reduced prices. Students can often get C$5 tickets. You can enjoy concerts in the *Roy Thomson Hall (tel. 416 8 72 42 55)* and opera or ballet in the city's new opera house, the *Four Seasons Centre (ticket sales from 11am on the day of the performance | 145 Queen St W | tel. 416 3 63 82 31 | coc.ca)*. In the beautifully renovated theatres of the theatre district you can catch top-quality West End and Broadway *musicals*.

Toronto has a great experimental theatre scene: 100-year old, female-managed *Alumnae Theatre Company (70 Berkeley St | alumnae theatre.com)* promotes young women in theatre, whereas the *Factory Theatre (125 Bathurst St | factorytheatre.ca)* programmes plays by young Canadian writers.

Chic *Yorkville*, *King Street* and especially *Queen Street* are popular among bar goers and music fans. The rooftop bar of the *Thompson Hotel (550 Wellington St W)* and the *Bar Raval (505 College St)* – inspired by Art Nouveau and Gaudí – in Little Italy, are both recommended for a drink. To watch sport with a beer in hand try the huge sports bar *Real Sports (15 York St)*.

For dancing visit *The Fifth Social Club (225 Richmond St W)* and the gay venue *Crews and Tangos (508 Church St)* known for its drag shows. Jazz is played at the *Rex Bar (194 Queen St)*, salsa at *Lula Lounge (1585 Dundas St. W, with dance classes)*, acid rock at the *Bovine Sex Club* bar *(542 Queen St)* and funky music at the *Rivoli* Thai restaurant *(334 Queen St W)* once visited by Amy Winehouse. Then there is classic rock at the *Horseshoe Tavern (370 Queen St W)*.

AROUND TORONTO

BLACK CREEK PIONEER VILLAGE

40km / 45 mins by car from Toronto on the Gardiner Expressway

The museum village north-west of Toronto recreates 19th-century pioneer life and there are special activities for children. *Daily in summer 10am–5pm, Sat/Sun from 11am | admission C$15, children C$11 | 1000 Murray Ross Parkway (close to Hwy 400) | blackcreek.ca | ⚏ E13*

MCMICHAEL CANADIAN ART COLLECTION ★

50km / 1 hr by car from Toronto on the Gardiner Expressway

The country's most important collection of Canadian art, focusing on native art (beautiful Inuit artworks) and paintings, including landscapes by the legendary *Group of Seven*. *Daily 10am–5pm, in winter Tue–Sun 10am–4pm | admission C$18 | 10365 Islington Ave | Kleinburg | mcmichael. com | ⚏ E13*

Black Creek Pioneer Village

ONTARIO

LAKES, ROCKS & WOODS

The First Nations gave the name Ontario – meaning *sparkling water* – to the massive region (approximately one million km²) extending between the Great Lakes and Hudson Bay.

Ontario is the second largest province in Canada (after Québec) and also the richest region in the country. It is a water-based holiday destination: there are old forts on the former canoe routes of the fur traders, fine sandy beaches on the shores of Lake Ontario, Lake Erie and Lake Huron, and, of course, the world-famous Niagara Falls.

Niagara Falls

The vast majority of the 14 million inhabitants (more than one-third of the country's total population) live in the south of the province in the greater metropolitan areas of Toronto and Hamilton. The scarcely populated north remains the domain of loggers and miners. Massive deposits of mineral resources lie in the hard rock of the Canadian Shield to the north, while in the mild, sunny climate in the south, agriculture, fruit orchards and vineyards flourish.

ONTARIO

Lake Nipigon

1400km, 16-17 hrs

● **Thunder Bay** P.66

Old Fort William ★

Lake Superior

MARCO POLO HIGHLIGHTS

★ **NIAGARA FALLS**
Spectacular natural wonder and tourist
attraction ➤ p. 54

★ **NIAGARA-ON-THE-LAKE**
Pioneer town that is touristy but pretty
➤ p. 56

★ **ST JACOBS**
Time travel to the land of the
Mennonites with their horse-drawn
carriages ➤ p. 57

★ **NATIONAL GALLERY OF CANADA**
Fantastic art in a great building
designed by Moshe Safdie ➤ p. 59

★ **CANADIAN MUSEUM OF HISTORY**
Treasures from all the regions of Canada
and some impressive totem poles
➤ p. 60

★ **ALGONQUIN PROVINCIAL PARK**
Ontario's most beautiful provincial park
and a canoeing paradise ➤ p. 63

★ **GEORGIAN BAY ISLANDS**
Visit the painters of the Group of Seven
in the wonderful world of the 30,000
Islands ➤ p. 64

★ **OLD FORT WILLIAM**
The world of the trappers and First
Nations preserved in an original fort
➤ p. 66

Sault Sainte Marie
p. 65

○ **Elliot
Lake**

Manitoulin Island
p. 64

Lake Michigan

○ **Traverse City**

U S A

Lake Huron

**Grand
Rapids** ○

Flint ○

Sarni

○ **Lansing**

Detroit ○ **Dresden**

○ **Kalamazoo**

**Point Pelee
Nat. Park**
p. 66

Point Pele
Beac

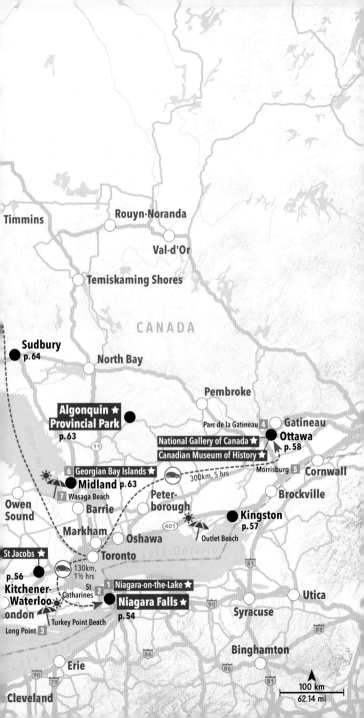

Timmins

Rouyn-Noranda

Val-d'Or

Temiskaming Shores

CANADA

Sudbury
p. 64

North Bay

Pembroke

Algonquin ★ Provincial Park
p. 63

Parc de la Gatineau **4**

Gatineau

National Gallery of Canada ★

Ottawa
p. 58

Canadian Museum of History ★

6 Georgian Bay Islands ★

Morrisburg **5**

Cornwall

Midland p. 63

300km, 5 hrs

7 Wasaga Beach

Peter-borough

Brockville

Owen Sound

Barrie

Kingston
p. 57

Markham

Outlet Beach

St Jacobs ★

Oshawa

Lake Ontario

p. 56

Toronto

Kitchener-Waterloo

130km, 1½ hrs

1 Niagara-on-the-Lake ★

Utica

ondon

St Catharines

2

Niagara Falls ★
p. 54

Syracuse

Long Point **3**

Turkey Point Beach

Binghamton

Erie

Cleveland

100 km
62.14 mi

NIAGARA FALLS

The thundering ⭐ 🐷 waterfalls on the Niagara River, which connects Lake Erie with Lake Ontario, are one of the greatest natural wonders of North America, and one that is also marketed relentlessly *(niagarafalls tourism.com)*.

Since the first white man, Jesuit missionary Louis Hennepin, saw the falls in 1678, much has changed. Two cities, both with the name *Niagara Falls*, lie on either side of the river which forms the border between Canada and the United States. Between them the falls plunge down, surrounded by gardens and protected as a national park.

All around is the tourist hustle and bustle that accompanies such attractions: neon exhibits, a waxworks museum, roller coasters, water parks and all sorts of souvenirs. Many of these take their names from the falls, such as the *Niagara Falls Adventure Theatre (niagarafallsmovie.com)* with its IMAX movie where you can experience the falls and the daredevil exploits that they have inspired cinematically. ⌸ *E13*

SIGHTSEEING

HORSESHOE/AMERICAN FALLS
The 54-m-high Canadian *Horseshoe Falls* are much more impressive than the 56-m-high and 323-m-wide *American Falls*.

The most beautiful viewing spot on the Canadian side is at *Table Rock House* and on the American side at *Luna Island*. At night the falls glow with colourful illumination.

HORNBLOWER NIAGARA CRUISES
Boat tours to the foot of the thundering waterfalls are a wet, but amazing experience. *Daily in summer, closed in winter due to ice | fare C$26 | departure at Clifton Hill St | niagaracruises.com*

TABLE ROCK/NIAGARA'S FURY/ JOURNEY BEHIND THE FALLS ▐
At the Canadian end of the falls a lift takes you below the waterfall's gushing edge, while a 360-degree cinema illustrates its dramatic origins. *In summer 9am–10pm, otherwise until 5.30pm | group tickets including shuttle bus C$25*

INSIDER TIP
It doesn't ge any closer o noisier!

WHIRLPOOL JETBOAT TOURS 🌴 👧
A splashing adventure for teenagers and parents alike: a wild one-hour boat tour through the rapids on the Niagara River below the falls. Be prepared for a tough ride and bring dry clothes for changing into afterwards. *Admission C$70, children C$45 | 3850 Niagara Parkway | tel. 905 4 68 48 00 | whirlpooljet.com*

EATING & DRINKING

BRAVO!
Perfect after a long sightseeing tour:

As close as you can get to the gigantic Niagara Falls!

great pizza and a huge selection of beers. *5438 Ferry St | tel. 905 3 54 33 54 | C$$*

MASSIMO'S

For special occasions: fine Italian cuisine, great wine – an elegant restaurant for dinner with marvellous views of the falls. *In the Sheraton on the Falls | 5875 Falls Ave | tel. 866 3 74 44 08 | C$$-$$$*

QUEENSTON HEIGHTS

Beautifully located terrace restaurant, a 15-minute drive downstream on the Niagara Parkway. Sunday brunch. *Queenston Heights Park | tel. 905 2 62 42 74 | C$$*

SKYLON DINING ROOM

Revolving restaurant in the 160-m-tall observation tower with panoramic views of the falls. *Tel. 905 3 56 26 51 | C$$*

SMOKE'S POUTINERIE

Try *poutine*, a typically Canadian fast-food classic in the midst of the tourist hype. *5869 Victoria Ave | tel. 905 3 56 28 73 | C$$*

SHOPPING

CANADA ONE FACTORY OUTLETS

Not quite as big or cheap as in the US, but still more than 40 companies offering discounted goods. *Daily 10am–9pm, Sun in winter until 6pm | 7500 Lundy's Lane*

AROUND NIAGARA

1 NIAGARA-ON-THE-LAKE ★

20km / 30 mins by car from Niagara City along the Niagara River

The drive north alone, along the *Niagara Parkway* past the *Botanical Gardens*, is worthwhile. The small town where the Niagara River joins Lake Ontario delights with pretty, historic brick buildings and Victorian façades from the 19th century. The famous Shaw Festival runs here for the whole summer. All around the town are large vineyards, belonging to wineries such as Jackson-Triggs, Peller, Strewn or *Reif Winery (daily 10am–6pm | 156089 Niagara Parkway | reifwinery.com)*. You

> **INSIDER TIP**
> **Traditional German wines**

just have to taste the ice wine which grows so well on the Niagara Peninsula. Many wineries provide picnic tables and benches. ⊞ E13

2 ST CATHARINES

20km / 30 mins by car from Niagara City on the QEW

Grapes, peaches, strawberries and vegetables flourish in the mild climate of the Niagara Peninsula. In its centre lies St Catharines, surrounded by fruit orchards. The town celebrates its agricultural produce with several festivals in spring and autumn. At locks Nos 3 and 7 on the Welland Canal you can watch the St Lawrence Seaway's extremely busy shipping traffic. ⊞ E13

3 LONG POINT 😀

130km / 2 hrs by car on country roads from Niagara City

This sports, adventure and nature centre with a beautiful 🏖 beach in the *Turkey Point Provincial Park* offers a great zipline with rope bridges and treetop trail. There are also kayak and bicycle tours, luxury tents and cabin hire. *Long Point Eco-Adventures | 1730 Front Rd | Turkey Point | tel. 877 7 43 86 87 | lpfun.ca | ⊞ E13*

KITCHENER– WATERLOO

The twin cities (pop. 525,000, *explorewaterlooregion.com*) are known throughout Canada for their high-tech industries and insurance company headquarters, as well as Kitchener's German heritage.

The fertile farmland west of Toronto has been a stronghold of German settlers for 200 years and schnitzel and sauerkraut are on many menus. Maypoles and glockenspiels decorate the main streets, while the farmer's market offers sausages and dark rye bread. The bustling city does not hide its background. Up until World War I, Kitchener was called Berlin. English is the main language, yet every autumn the descendants of the immigrants remember their roots, and celebrate a big Oktoberfest.

The idyllic countryside north of Kitchener shows the different lifestyle of the German pioneers. Deeply religious Mennonites live here. Between *Heidelberg*, *Elmira* and *Elora* you see them on the highway in old-fashioned horse-drawn carriages.

In ⭐ *St Jacobs* the visitor centre highlights their religion. At the big *farmer's market (in summer Tue, Thu and Sat | Hwy 85, Exit Rd 15)* families sell vegetables, jams and excellent sausages. The beef "summer sausages" are every bit as good as European salamis. Next door, an outlet mall tempts contemporary shoppers. *F13*

EATING & DRINKING

STONE CROCK RESTAURANT

Sample German-Mennonite cuisine. The adjoining bakery produces heavenly *pies. 1396 King St N | tel. 519 6 64 22 86 | C$$*

KINGSTON

Many young people live in the old garrison town (pop. 170,000, *visit kingston.ca*) which has a large marina and is home to several colleges, including the prestigious Queen's University.

The city, founded in 1673 as a fur-trading post where the St Lawrence River flows from Lake Ontario, is keen to preserve its history. The typical blue-grey limestone was used to construct many buildings, which is how Kingston got its nickname "Limestone City". South-west of the city, sand awaits you in the *Sandbanks Provincial Park* with its wide child-friendly *Outlet Beach* and dunes. *G13*

Lively Niagara-on-the-Lake makes a great day out

Changing of the guard in Fort Henry by the St Lawrence

SIGHTSEEING

FORT HENRY

Cannons fire and soldiers in colourful uniforms drill in front of thick walls. Daily at 3pm history is re-enacted in the huge fortress above the St Lawrence river. The war of 1812 is the theme of the military museum. *End May–end Sept 9.45am–5pm | admission C$20 | 1 Fort Henry Dr. | forthenry. com | ⏱ 1 hr*

CANADA'S PENITENTIARY MUSEUM

The Penitentiary Museum is a bit gruesome. You can see old photos of cells and prison riots, tools and weapons used for breaking out and hear the stories of legendary prisoners. Book early (kingstonpentour.com) to take part in a guided tour of the high-security wing which was closed in 2013. *Summer 9am–6pm | admission free, donations requested | 555 King St | penitentiarymuseum.ca*

INSIDER TIP
Guided tours of Canada's Alcatraz

ISLAND QUEEN

Boat tours to the island labyrinth of the Thousand Islands. *Departure from Crawford Dock | tickets C$35-88 | tel. 613 5 49 55 44 | 1000islandscruises.ca*

OTTAWA

Canada's capital (pop. 1.4 million, *ottawatourism.ca*) on the Ottawa River is famous for its quality of life which merges British and French elements.

Although it is the coldest capital – temperature-wise – in the Western world, it is also one of the cleanest. There are no air-polluting industries; Ottawa's only job is to govern the nation.

British traditions such as the ceremonial changing of the guard in front of parliament (*daily in summer 10am*) remain popular tourist attractions. However, the French lifestyle has spilt over the Ottawa River from Québec and changed the once-sleepy capital into a vibrant metropolis.

There is no shortage of culture in the city, which has a modern *National Arts Centre* with an opera house and various museums. And you can relax in the cafés around the colourful *Byward Market* or in one of the parks along the flower-lined Rideau Canal, which traverses the city centre like a Dutch canal. *G12*

SIGHTSEEING

PARLIAMENT HILL

High above the southern banks of the Ottawa River, Canada's Parliament occupies the city's most prominent position. Construction of the neo-Gothic *Parliament* began in 1859, two years after Queen Victoria declared the remote lumberjack camp of *Bytown* the new capital, thus destroying the hopes of Montréal and Toronto. Within a few years it became a "Westminster in the wilderness". *Daily in summer at 9.45am ceremonial changing of the guard and evening 🐦 son et lumière shows | interior closed until 2028 due to renovation work*

You have the best views from *Nepean Point* behind the National Gallery where a monument to Samuel de Champlain looks out over the Ottawa River. He was the first white man to travel here in 1613. *G12*

BYWARD MARKET

Established in 1826, with its market stalls, street cafés and trendy bars, Byward Market is the best place to experience the city's lifestyle. Try Ottawa's speciality *beavertails* 0150 delicious fried dough pastry – at the baker's stand. *Killaloe Sunrise* with lemon is recommended. *George St/Byward Market Square | byward-market.com*

INSIDER TIP
Delicious beavertails

NATIONAL GALLERY OF CANADA ★

Excellent Canadian art, including marvellous Inuit sculptures, is

---

WHERE TO START?

The changing of the guard takes place at 9.45am at the **Parliament**. It's a good starting point and there are many attractions nearby. Across the Rideau Canal and past the Château Laurier you will reach Nepean Point for a fabulous view of the city and the Ottawa River. Nearby are the National Gallery and the lively district around Byward Market.
Parking is on York St or in the car park by George St/Byward Market. Buses 1, 2, 7, 9, 12

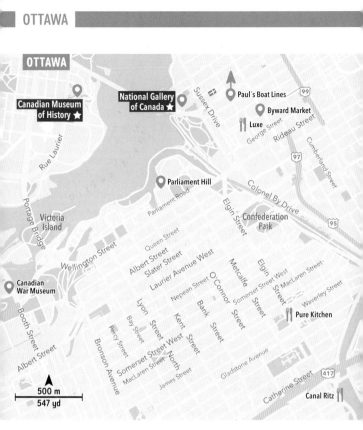

OTTAWA

Canadian Museum of History ★

National Gallery of Canada ★

Sussex Drive

Paul's Boat Lines 99

Byward Market

Luxe

George Street

Rideau Street

Cumberland Street

Rue Laurier

97

Parliament Hill

Colonel By Drive

Rideau Canal

Parliament Road

Elgin Street

Confederation Park

95

Portage Bridge

Victoria Island

Queen Street

Albert Street

Slater Street

Laurier Avenue West

Metcalfe

Elgin Street

Somerset Street West

MacLaren Street

Wellington Street

Nepean Street

O'Connor Street

Street

Somerset Street

Waverley Street

Canadian War Museum

Lyon Street

Bay Street

Kent Street

Bank Street

Pure Kitchen

Booth Street

Percy Street

Bronson Avenue

Somerset Street West

MacLaren Street

James Street

North

Gladstone Avenue

Catherine Street

417

Albert Street

500 m
547 yd

Canal Ritz

exhibited in a building designed by Moshe Safdie. There are also European highlights from Rubens and the giant spider by Louise Bourgeois. *Daily in summer 10am–6pm, otherwise Tue–Sun 10am–5pm, Thu always until 8pm | admission C$15 | 380 Sussex Dr. | gallery.ca | ⊙ 2 hrs*

CANADIAN MUSEUM OF HISTORY ★

This is spectacular architecture on the northern banks of the Ottawa River. The curved forms and materials used emulate the landscapes and cultures of Canada, as intended by indigenous architect Douglas Cardinal. This, the most-visited museum in the country, opened in 1989 and houses excellent exhibitions on First Nation and Inuit cultures in Canada and on the frontier history. Interesting: the multi-storey entrance hall with totem poles.

INSIDER TIP
Beautifully carved totem poles

The adjacent Canadian Children's Museum displays the country's many multicultural elements, including toys from across the world and a colourful bus from Pakistan. *Daily 9.30am–5pm, in summer until 6pm, Thu always until 8pm |*

admission C$20, children C$12, families C$50 | Gatineau | 100 Laurier St | historymuseum.ca | ⏱ 3 hrs

CANADIAN WAR MUSEUM

A spectacular new building above the Ottawa River with good exhibitions depicting Canada's role in UN peacekeeping forces. *Daily 9.30am–5pm, Thu until 8pm | admission C$17 | 1 Vimy Place | warmuseum.ca | ⏱ 2 hrs*

PAUL'S BOAT LINES

Sightseeing trips on the Ottawa River and Rideau Canal. *Departure: Ottawa Locks and Hulls Marina in Gatineau | fare C$27 | tel. 613 2 25 67 81 | paulsboatline.com*

EATING & DRINKING

CANAL RITZ

Just outside the centre in a beautiful setting on the *Rideau Canal*. Delicious mussels, salads and pasta. *375 Queen Elizabeth Dr. | tel. 613 2 38 89 98 | C$$*

LUXE

Good steaks, a nice terrace and perfect location by Byward Market. *47 York St | tel. 619 2 41 88 05 | C$$*

PURE KITCHEN

Everything is organic and fresh in this fashionable vegetarian restaurant: soups and tasty sandwiches plus fruit juice, gluten-free beer and delicious

Reminders of Europe: Ottawa's library and the mighty Parliament building

First Nation and Inuit art in the Canadian Museum of History

Colonel By Dr.) has over 200 shops. The pedestrian zone *Sparks Street Mall* is filled with small bookstores, galleries and boutiques.

NIGHTLIFE

Theatre, ballet and concert performances are held in the *National Arts Centre (tel. 613 9 47 70 00 | nac-cna. ca)*. Popular meeting spots are venues such as *Pub 101 (101 York St)* at Byward Market, the very British *Heart & Crown Pub (67 Clarence St)* and the *Rainbow Bistro (76 Murray St)*. In summer, Ottawa's *National Capital Commission (ncc-ccn.gc.ca)* organises 🍂 mostly free concerts and theatre performances in the parks.

AROUND OTTAWA

4 PARC DE LA GATINEAU
15km / 20 mins by car from Ottawa
Bicycle lanes and scenic roads crisscross the 360km² of this large park filled with forests and lakes on the northern banks of the Ottawa River outside town. The viewing spots are especially beautiful during the "Indian Summer" from the end of September. *Visitor centre in Chelsea | access from Hwy 5 | 🗺 G12*

5 MORRISBURG
90km / 1.5 hrs by car from Ottawa on country roads
During the construction of the St

cocktails. *340 Elgin St | tel. 613 2 33 78 73 | C$-$$*

SHOPPING

The most attractive shopping district is the old town around *Byward Market*, with speciality stores and art galleries. The *Rideau Centre (corner of Rideau St/*

Lawrence Seaway, the village of Morrisburg (pop. 2,500) was forcibly moved to the river's new, higher bank. The 35 houses of the loyalist settlers were rebuilt in the museum village *Upper Canada Village (daily in summer 9.30am–5pm | admission C$18 | uppercanadavillage.com | ⏱ 3 hrs)* on Hwy 2. Experience everyday life in 1880 where farmers plough with oxen and yarn is spun in the living room.

North of the village, the Long Sault Parkway scenic road leads past pretty swimming spots and viewing points, overlooking the eleven islands in the St Lawrence. *□ G12*

INSIDER TIP
idyllic life by the great river

ALGONQUIN PROVINCIAL PARK

Canoeists and hikers can look forward to the oldest nature reserve in Ontario, the ★ ⚑ Algonquin Provincial Park – a 7,600-km² region of forests and lakes and home to moose, black bears and beavers.

The park is easily accessible, with numerous short nature trails through typical Canadian forest leading off Hwy 60. There are 1,600km of canoe routes leading into the remote hinterland. The *visitor centre* on Hwy 60 includes a museum and provides maps. Canoe and equipment hire

(including guided tours) are available at *Algonquin Outfitters (Oxtongue Lake | Dwight | tel. 800 4 69 49 48 | algonquinoutfitters.com).*

In the south-west of Algonquin Park, a two-hour drive from its western entrance, is the *Haliburton Forest* eco-centre *(daily in summer 8am–5pm | admission C$25 | haliburtonforest. com),* with a wolf enclosure and treetop nature trail including camping, cabin and canoe hire. *□ F11–12*

MIDLAND

This resort town (pop. 16,000, midland.ca) and water sports centre is on the southern shore of Georgian Bay. Here, in the ancestral region of the Hurons, the Jesuits founded a mission in 1639 – with limited success: eight missionaries died at the stake.

The *Huronia Museum (daily in summer 9am–5pm, otherwise closed Sat/ Sun | admission C$12 | Little Lake Park)* has exhibits about the history of the Hurons and a replica village. *□ E12*

SIGHTSEEING

SAINTE-MARIE AMONG THE HURONS

Sainte-Marie among the Hurons is a living museum *(Huronia Museum)* and an impressive reconstruction of the Jesuit mission from 1639 *(daily in summer 10am–5pm, otherwise closed*

INSIDER TIP
Experience the real deal

Sat/Sun | admission C$12 | Little Lake Park | Hwy 12).

DISCOVERY HARBOUR 👥

The museum harbour on the shores of Lake Huron has an extensive participative programme from making model ships and learning about knots to raiding old sailing ships. *End of June–Sept 10am–5pm | admission C$7, children C$5.25 | 93 Jury Dr. | Penetanguishene/Midland | discovery harbour.on.ca | ⏱ 2 hrs | ▭ E12*

AROUND MIDLAND

⑥ GEORGIAN BAY ISLANDS ★
15km / 2.5 hrs boat trip from Midland

The wildly romantic island group in the south-eastern Georgian Bay was made famous by the Group of Seven's paintings. The group was inspired by the granite rocks and windswept trees on the small islands. Boat tours and water taxis are available. *Departure from Midland on the "Miss Midland" (fare C$36 | tel. 705 5 49 33 88 | midlandtours.com) and in Honey Harbour at the end of Hwy 5 | ▭ E12*

⑦ WASAGA BEACH
40km / 30 mins from Midland

Very popular holiday resort with a 🏖 14-km-long sandy beach south-west of Midland. Water parks, minigolf, nice holiday motels: summer beach fun. *▭ E12*

SUDBURY

Compasses go wild in the Sudbury Basin, not pointing north, but instead down to the earth! This is due to the huge metal deposits underground, including nickel, copper, iron, silver and cobalt, allegedly originating from a meteorite impact two billion years ago.

This makes Sudbury the most important mining town in northern Ontario (pop. 165,000). The *Science North* museum *(daily in summer 9am–4pm | admission C$27, children C$23 | sciencenorth.ca | ⏱ 3 hrs)* demonstrates mining techniques in the "Dynamic Earth" exhibition, including a virtual tour of a mine.

INSIDER TIP
Mining – virtual and state of the art

A popular area for canoeists is the *Killarney Provincial Park (canoe rentals at the park entrance)* on the shores of Georgian Bay, south of the city. *▭ E11*

MANITOULIN ISLAND

Five First Nation reservations are situated on the 176-km-long island in Lake Huron, the world's largest island in a freshwater lake.

The small reservation towns sell woven grass baskets decorated with porcupine quills and other craft items made by the *Ojibwa*. A big *pow-wow* is

On Manitoulin Island a great museum explains Ojibwa culture

held in early August. For information about festivals, attractions and Native American tours in the region visit the *Great Spirit Circle Trail* website *(circletrail.com).* C–D11

SAULT SAINTE MARIE

The industrial and harbour city of Sault Sainte Marie (pop. 73,000, *algomacountry.com***) lies on the border with the US, at the narrow point between Lake Superior and Lake Huron. It is a good starting point for tours to the hinterland,** **the rugged coast of Lake Superior and lakes that are rich in fish.**

The mighty rapids, where the Jesuits founded a mission in 1669, are circumvented by the St Lawrence Seaway's impressive *canal lock system (boat trips from the US-side).* In the *Canadian Bushplane Heritage Centre (mid May–mid Oct 9am–6pm, otherwise 10am–4pm | admission C$13.50 | 50 Pim St | bushplane.com)* you can view 20 historic aircraft and explore the era of bush flying. Especially lovely during the autumn are the day-excursions by train to the Agawa Canyon with the *Algoma Central Railway (129 Bay St | tel. 705 9 46 73 00 | agawatrain.com).* C10–11

THUNDER BAY

The city (pop. 120,000, *thunderbay. ca*) on the north-western shore of Lake Superior is situated in the centre of the continent and has the third-largest harbour in Canada.

Many of the massive grain silos in the harbour are now empty because the grain from the prairies that was shipped via the St Lawrence Seaway to the Atlantic, 3,700km away, is now increasingly transported to the Pacific. The *Centennial Park* on the Current River offers 30km of hiking and biking trails as well as logging exhibitions. *A9*

SIGHTSEEING

OLD FORT WILLIAM ★

On the south-western outskirts is a reconstructed 1816 fur-trading fort with 40 buildings, recreating the trapper days of Montréal's *North West Trading Company*. Gaze at a night sky free from light pollution above Thunder Bay from the adjoining *Astronomy Centre. Daily in summer 10am–5pm | admission C$14 | Broadway Ave | fwhp.ca | ⏱ 3 hrs*

POINT PELEE NATIONAL PARK

The southernmost point of Canada – roughly on the same latitude as Rome – is the best place for birdwatching in Eastern Canada.

Lake Erie – a favourite swimming spot for Canadians in the summer – has a 🪽 20-km sandbank where tens

Old Fort William

WHERE TO STAY IN ONTARIO

YOUNG & ECCENTRIC

Only a few streets from Ottawa's Parliament is the *Alt Hotel (148 rooms | 185 Slater St | tel. 613 6 91 68 82 | althotels.com | C$$)*, which has a cool industrial look and eccentric furniture.

A VIEW OF THE FALLS

You can't get closer to the Niagara Falls than in the *Oakes Hotel (6546 Fallsview Blvd | tel. 877 8 43 62 53 | oakeshotel.com | C$$)*. It is a little basic, but you are paying for the fabulous view from your room and the panorama lounge – perfect for the evening light show.

Ring-billed gulls in the Point Pelee National Park

of thousands of migratory birds gather in May and September.

Another fantastic spectacle of nature are the swarms of monarch butterflies that depart on their 3,000km journey to Mexico in mid-September. Amateur ornithologists might enjoy a day trip by boat to *Pelee Island*. ⌘ C14

INSIDER TIP
Migrating butterflies

AROUND POINT PELEE

8 DRESDEN

90km / 1.5 hrs from Point Pelee
The farming village (pop. 2,600) was a

destination of hope for slaves from the USA around 1850: the Underground Railroad ended there, a secret escape route for slaves fleeing from the Confederate States.

One of the refugees was Josiah Henson, on whom Harriet Beecher Stowe's novel *Uncle Tom's Cabin* was apparently based. Today, Henson's house is an interesting literary museum *(in summer Tue–Sat 10am–4pm, Sun noon–4pm | admission C$7 | Park St W | uncletomscabin. org)*. ⌘ D13

MONTRÉAL

GLOBAL CITY WITH CHARM

Montréal, Canada's second largest city with around 4.1 million citizens, has many sights and historical monuments to visit, but it's also a city that needs to be explored and experienced. Only then will you appreciate the true joie de vivre of the Montréalers and their diverse culture. In summer, when life revolves around the street cafés and parks around Mont Royal, the city is at its most enjoyable.

View from Mont Royal

The latest fashion, creative arts, bistros, bars and elegant boutiques – in Montréal *(mtl.org)* old and new worlds meet. Seventy per cent of the inhabitants speaks French, and the Gallic temperament – the enjoyment of good food and a chat in the bistro – is very much intact, despite 250 years of British affiliation. Closing time is not until 3am and Montréalers take full advantage of this.

MONTRÉAL

MARCO POLO HIGHLIGHTS

★ **POINTE-À-CALLIÈRE**
Multimedia show and ruins deep underground by the river ➤ p.73

★ **MONT ROYAL TERRACE**
Fantastic panoramic views over Montréal ➤ p.74

★ **PLATEAU MONT-ROYAL**
Young crowd, trendy shops, cafés and the best bagels ➤ p.74

★ **BIODÔME**
An ecological journey from rainforest to the Arctic in what was once a velodrome ➤ p.75

★ **SCHWARTZ'**
Almost an institution – many Montréalers are happy to queue for their spicy smoked meat ➤ p.77

★ **MARCHÉ JEAN-TALON**
A Parisian market could not be more beautiful – a real gourmet paradise with excellent regional produce ➤ p.77

★ **LAURENTIDES**
The most beautiful destination for an escape into the countryside is only an hour's drive from the city ➤ p.79

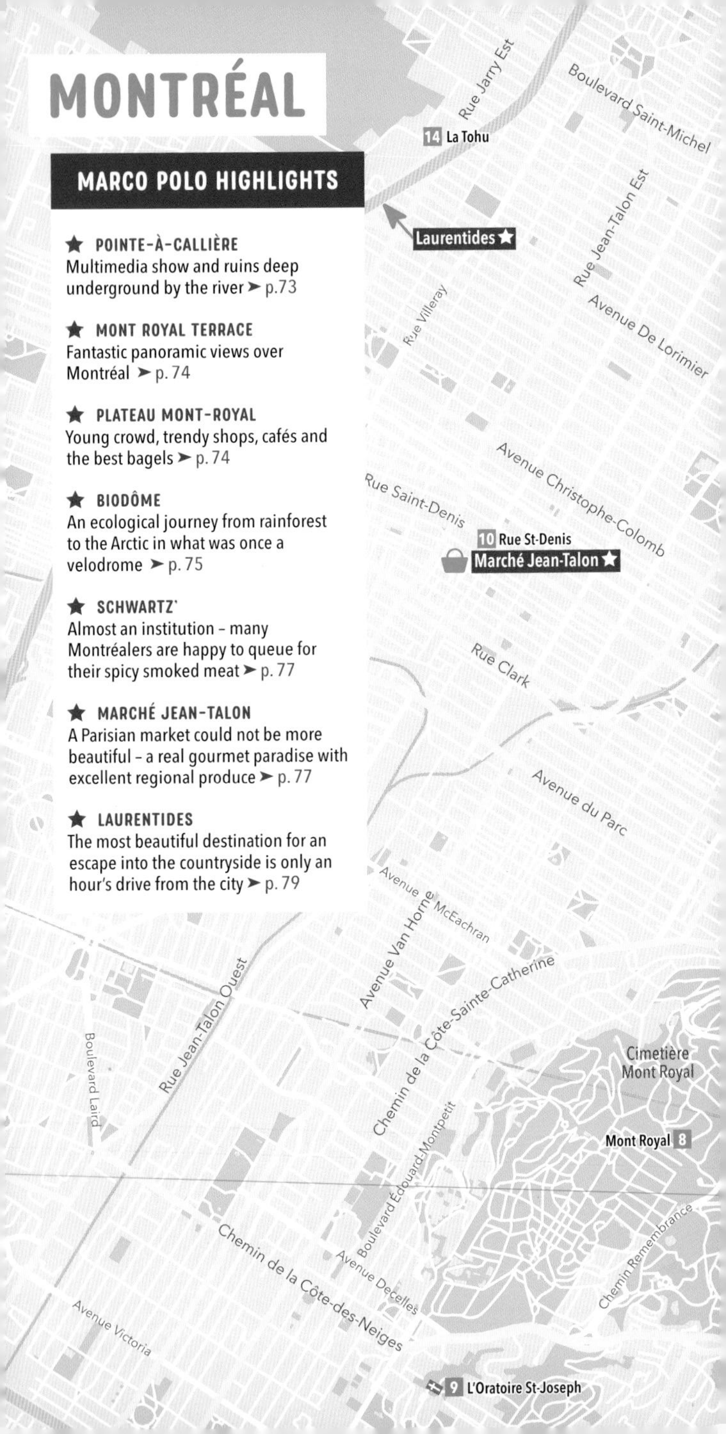

14 La Tohu

Boulevard Saint-Michel

Rue Jarry Est

Rue Jean-Talon Est

Laurentides ★

Rue Villeray

Avenue De Lorimier

Avenue Christophe-Colomb

Rue Saint-Denis

10 Rue St-Denis
Marché Jean-Talon ★

Rue Clark

Avenue du Parc

Avenue Van Horne

McEachran

Avenue de la Côte-Sainte-Catherine

Boulevard Édouard-Montpetit

Chemin de la Côte-Sainte-Catherine

Boulevard Laird

Rue Jean-Talon Ouest

Cimetière Mont Royal

Mont Royal 8

Chemin Remembrance

Chemin de la Côte-des-Neiges

Avenue Decelles

Avenue Victoria

9 L'Oratoire St-Joseph

11 Jardin Botanique

13 Biodôme ★

12 Parc Olympique

Rue Viau

Rue Sherbrooke Est

Boulevard Pie-IX

Rue Ontario Est

Rue Sainte-Catherine Est

Rue de Bellechasse

Boulevard Rosémont

Rue D'Iberville

Rue Davidson

Rue Hochelaga

Rue Notre-Dame Est

Fleuve

Avenue Laurier Est

Boulevard Saint-Joseph Est

Avenue De Lorimier

Rue Rachel Est

Rue Frontenac

Avenue Papineau

Avenue De Lorimier

Parc
La Fontaine

Rue Sherbrooke Est

Avenue du Mont-Royal Est

Boulevard De Maisonneuve Est

Pont Jacques-Cartier

Plateau Mont-Royal ★

Rue Saint-Denis

Rue Ontario Est

Rue Berri

Boulevard René-Lévesque Est

Île Ste-Hélène **15**

Parc
Jeanne Mance

Saint

Schwartz' ★ | Moishe's

Chez Cora

Avenue du Parc

Rue Saint-Urbain

Resto Vego

Maestro S.V.P.

Plage Tour de l'Horloge

Parc du
Mont-Royal

Rue University

Musée d'Art
Contemporain **4**

Chez L'Epicier

Vieux Montréal **1**

Musée McCord **5**

Ville
Souterraine/
RÉSO

Pont Royal Terrace ★

2 Pointe-à-Callière ★

Barbie Expo **6**
Firegrill

XO
Le Restaurant

Boulevard Robert-Bourassa

Avenue Pierre-Dupuy

Pont de la Concorde

Laurent

Musée des
Beaux-Arts **7**

Ouest

Rue Peel

3 Rue Ste-Catherine

Marché Atwater

Rue Sherbrooke

Rue Guy

Montréal

750 m
820 yd

MONTRÉAL

The traders and travellers set forth from Montréal into the forests of the west and the north, conquering the continent. It was the last port along the St Lawrence – the rapids above the settlement could not be navigated. Today these rapids are still called *Lachine*, because the discoverer Jacques Cartier believed that they led to the Northwest Passage and China. In the 19th century, Montréal quickly became Canada's most important city. Today it is Eastern Canada's second, and livelier, metropolis and it is not going to give up its French-Canadian lifestyle.

SIGHTSEEING

Finding your way around Montréal is straightforward. On the southern banks of the Île de Montréal lies the old town *(Vieux Montréal)*, full of nooks and crannies and cobbled streets. Behind it are the skyscrapers of the city itself, gently sloping towards the river between the old town and Mont Royal. To the west is the residential and shopping district of *Westmount* where English is mostly spoken.

Boulevard St-Laurent, a predominantly immigrant neighbourhood, runs north-east of the city centre, and the French quarter begins beyond, on Rue St-Denis.

You can enjoy city tours with regular sightseeing buses, e.g. *Grayline Tours*

WHERE TO START?

Start at the **Place Jacques Cartier** (⏛ e3) in the heart of the winding old town, with the Basilique Notre-Dame and the bustling piers of the harbour nearby. From here, by metro or bicycle, you can reach the Rue Ste-Catherine shopping thoroughfare, the Musée des Beaux-Arts or the fashionable Rue St-Denis in the Plateau Mont-Royal district.
There is ample parking on Rue de la Commune, east of Place Jacques-Cartier.

(tel. 514 3 98 97 69), and boat tours of the harbour, e.g. *Croisères AML (tel. 866 8 56 66 68)* and *Bateau Mouche (tel. 514 8 49 99 52)*.

The 🐷 *Montreal Museums Pass* offers three days' admission to all museums for C$75. If you pay another C$5, buses and trains are free as well.

1 VIEUX MONTRÉAL

The most important attractions of the old town lie around the Place Jacques Cartier and Place d'Armes: the *Basilique Notre-Dame* (evening son et lumière show), the *Chapelle Notre-Dame-de-Bonsecours* and the *Château de Ramezay*, once the governor's residence, today a museum of the city's history. There is also the classical domed building of the *Marché Bonsecours* on Rue St-Paul, which has frequent exhibitions. And by the river the piers of the *Vieux Port* lure visitors with an IMAX cinema, flea markets,

Neo-Gothic splendour from 1843: Basilique Notre-Dame in Vieux Montréal

boat trips and summer festivals. *Plage Tour de l'Horloge* is a sandy beach at the end of the pier. If you feel energetic, you can climb the 192 steps of this historic tower (admission free). If you're tired of walking, there are massages or spa treatments in the five-storey *Bota Bota Spa (botabota.ca)* on a refurbished old ferry in the old harbour to the south. 🖾 *d–e3*

2 POINTE-À-CALLIÈRE ★

City history with a difference: after a spectacular multimedia introduction you can walk underneath the Place Royale in a subterranean labyrinth of old ruins, past the city's first cemetery, an early tavern and the foundations of the first settlers' fort. *Mon–Fri 10am–6pm, Sat/Sun 11am–6pm,* otherwise *Tue–Sun until 5pm | admission C$22 | 350, Place Royale | pacmusee.qc.ca | ⏱ 1 hr | 🖾 e*

3 RUE STE-CATHERINE

Shopping, eating, looking: this is the city centre's main thoroughfare. On the southern side of *Dorchester Square* (tourist information) is the *Cathédrale Marie-Reine-du-Monde*, a scale replica of St Peter's in Rome. 🖾 *a–e 6–1*

4 MUSÉE D'ART CONTEMPORAIN

Contemporary Québec artists are showcased in an extensive postmodern building. Good bookshop. *Tue 11am–6pm, Mon–Fri 11am–9pm, Sat/Sun 10am–6pm | admission C$17 | 185, Rue Ste-Catherine Ouest | macm. org | ⏱ 1–2 hrs | 🖾 c–d3*

5 MUSÉE MCCORD

This small museum tells the history of Canada and has some fine First Nation beadwork. *Daily in summer 10am–6pm, Wed until 9pm, Sat/Sun until 5pm, during the winter closed Mon | admission C$19 | 690, Rue Sherbrooke Ouest | mccord-museum. qc.ca | ⊙ 1 hr | ◫ c3*

6 BARBIE EXPO 🐷 🎭

Wonderfully crazy and unique: 1,000 Barbie dolls wearing designer clothes by Dior and Armani. This must be the largest Barbie exhibition in the world. *Open daily 10am–7pm, Thu/Fri until 9pm, Sun 10am–5pm | admission free | 1455, Rue Peel in the Les Cours Mont-Royal | ◫ c4*

7 MUSÉE DES BEAUX-ARTS

Canada's oldest art museum is famous for its special exhibitions in the new building by Canadian architect Moshe Safdie. Good museum shop. *Tue–Thu 10am–5pm, special exhibition Wed until 9pm | admission free for people under 30, otherwise C$15; special exhibition C$23, under 30 C$15 | 1380, Rue Sherbrooke Ouest | mbam.qc.ca | ⊙ 2 hrs | ◫ b4*

8 MONT ROYAL

The mountain that gave Montréal its name is today a 2-km² forested park. From the Mont Royal's *Grand Chalet* ★ *terrace* you will have fantastic views of the city skyline. The *visitor centre (daily 9am–6pm | 1260 Remembrance Rd) in Smith House* in the centre of the park has a restaurant with a terrace that is ideal for a break.

In the park's north-east corner, by the *George Étienne Cartier Monument*, drummers meet every Sunday in summer for *Tam-Tams* – freestyle dancing and drumming performances. *◫ a2–3*

9 L'ORATOIRE ST-JOSEPH

Québecers are traditionally Catholics and this basilica, dedicated to the miracle healer Frère André, is their place of pilgrimage. The massive dome of the 97-m-tall basilica is the second highest in the world after St Peter's. *Daily 7am–9pm, carillon Wed–Fri noon and 3pm, Sat/Sun noon and 2.30pm | 3800, Chemin Queen Mary | ◫ H12*

10 RUE ST-DENIS

Street cafés, cinemas and small restaurants characterise the area around the *Université du Québec*. To the north-west, at the intersection with Avenue du Mont-Royal, the lively ★ *Plateau Mont-Royal* district starts. Today, funky boutiques and bistros reside in the brick buildings of former immigrants. Tip for refreshments: a bagel in the *St-Viateur* bakery *(1127, Ave du Mont-Royal Est). ◫ c–e 1–2*

11 JARDIN BOTANIQUE

Montréal's botanical garden ranks as one of the best in the world. There are Japanese and Indian gardens as well as a fascinating 🎭 *insectarium* where you can admire beetles, caterpillars, butterflies and spiders. *Daily in summer 9am–6pm, otherwise Tue–Sun*

9am–5pm | admission C$20.25, incl. Biodôme C$3.5 | 4101, Rue Sherbrooke Est | espacepourlavie.ca | ▢ H12

12 PARC OLYMPIQUE

Rising above the 1976 Olympic stadium is the dramatic 165m leaning tower, one of the city's most popular attractions. The spectacular tower, with its 45 degree angle, was only completed 11 years after the Olympic Games following numerous construction scandals. The view from the observation deck is best in the morning and at night. *Daily in summer 9am–6pm, Mon from 1pm, in winter until 5pm | admission C$23.75 | 4141, Av. Pierre-de-Coubertin | ▢ H12*

13 BIODÔME ★ 👥

The former *Parc Olympique* velodrome today houses an eco-museum that includes replicas of the four most important ecosystems of the American continent, including rainforests and Arctic ice caves. *Daily in summer 9am–6pm, otherwise Tue–Sun 9am–5pm | admission C$20.50, children C$10.50, incl. Jardin Botanique C$35 | 4777, Av. Pierre de Coubertin | espacepourlavie.ca | ▢ H12*

14 LA TOHU 👥

This circus school and training centre for Cirque du Soleil was built to eco-friendly standards on what was once a rubbish dump. Innovative circus performances are often programmed:

Lantern festival in the vast Chinese garden of the Jardin Botanique

A relic of the Expo 1967, the Biosphère dome is now dedicated to ecology

Guided tours daily 9am–5pm | 2345, Rue Jarry Est | tel. 514 3 76 86 48 | tohu.ca | ▥ *H12*

15 ÎLE STE-HÉLÈNE

The parks of the small island off the old town are popular with Montréalers. There is the 🐒 *La Ronde* amusement park and an old *fort* dating back to 1822 (with military museum) where soldiers in historical costumes parade in summer. On the wet of the island after sunset, the Jacques Cartier Bridge is illuminated according to the city's rhythmic cycle.

INSIDER TIP
Nightlife of a bridge

Expo 67 took place in the southern part of the island and on neighbouring *Île Notre-Dame*. Some of its surviving buildings include the former French pavilion with *casino* and the huge 🐒 *Biosphère (daily in summer 10am–5pm, in winter closed Thu/Tue | admission C\$15, children C\$10 | ec.gc.ca/biosphere)* – once the US pavilion – with exhibitions on ecology, climate and water and air quality. Île Notre-Dame is also where Montréal's *Grand Prix racing circuit* is situated. ▥ *H12*

EATING & DRINKING

In the *Plateau Quarter* and around *Rue Prince-Arthur* and *Rue Duluth* many of the cheaper restaurants allow you to bring your own wine *(apportez votre vin, BYOW)*. The restaurants provide glasses for a small fee.

CHEZ CORA 🦃

A franchise of cosy snack bars, serving Montréal's most popular and cheapest breakfast with fruit, waffles, pancakes and muesli. *1240, Rue Drummond (also 1017, Rue Ste-Catherine Est) | chezcora.com | C$ | ⚏ c4*

CHEZ L'EPICIER

Modern, innovative Québecois cuisine in the middle of the historic centre with an interior styled as a grocery store. *311, Rue St-Paul Est | tel. 514 8 78 22 32 | C$$$ | ⚏ e3*

FIREGRILL

If you like meat dishes, you'll enjoy the thick *striploin* steaks and juicy *firegrill* burgers. Close to the nightlife district around the Rue Crescent in the west of the city. *1490, Rue Stanley | tel. 514 8 42 00 20 | C$$-$$$ | ⚏ b–c4*

MAESTRO S.V.P.

This bistro offers dozens of oyster and shellfish dishes, many originating in the Atlantic provinces of Canada, and all are on view in the huge display case at the entrance. *3615, Blvd St-Laurent | tel. 514 8 42 64 47 | C$$ | ⚏ c2*

MOISHE'S

A steakhouse steeped in tradition where Leonard Cohen used to dine several times a week. *3961, Blvd St-Laurent | tel. 514 8 45 35 09 | C$ | ⚏ b–c1*

RESTO VEGO 🐷

Small chain of vegetarian buffet restaurants with several branches in the city, e.g. in the centre of the student district, with pleasant terraces: *1720, Rue St-Denis | tel. 514 8 45 26 27 | C$ | ⚏ d1–2*

SCHWARTZ' ⭐

This classic Yiddish deli restaurant is famous for its smoked meat. For C$10 you can enjoy a hearty *smoked meat sandwich*; for C$18 a giant platter. *3895, Blvd St-Laurent | tel. 514 8 42 48 13 | C$ | ⚏ b–c1*

XO LE RESTAURANT

Ideal for an elegant dinner or a sophisticated Sunday brunch: fine French-Canadian cuisine served in the hall of an old bank. *355, Rue St-Jacques Ouest | tel. 514 8 41 50 00 | C$$$ | ⚏ d4*

SHOPPING

MARCHÉ ATWATER

A beautiful market on the English south-west side of the city. Opposite is the Lachine Canal – great for walking and bicycling. *From 8am | 138 Atwater Av. | ⚏ H12*

MARCHÉ JEAN-TALON ⭐

The most attractive of Montréal's markets: from 7am there's lots of scrambling and jostling round the mountains of apples and artichokes. Excellent Québec products such as jams and liqueurs can be found at *Le Marché des Saveurs. 7070 Ave Henri-Julien | ⚏ H12*

VILLE SOUTERRAINE/RÉSO ☂

A weatherproof underground city that is a series of interconnected complexes totalling 30km. 200 restaurants, 50 banks, 40 cinemas, theatres, concert halls and 2,000 shops form part of the air-conditioned labyrinth in the

DESIGN TEMPLE

A pilgrimage site for design fans. The historic Beaux Arts façade of the *Hotel Gault (30 rooms | 449, Rue Ste-Hélène | tel. 514 9 04 16 16 | hotelgault.com | C$$$ | ▥ e3)* gives no indication of the avant-garde design inside: 1960s furniture (chairs by Pierre Paulin), futuristic lighting, polished wood floors and raw concrete walls.

COSY GUESTHOUSE

Cheerful yellow walls, narrow hallways, stairs and balconies transform the *Anne Ma Soeur Anne guesthouse (17 rooms | 4119, Rue St-Denis | tel. 514 2 81 31 87 | annemasoeuranne.com | C$-$$ | ▥ b1)* into a labyrinth. But this is exactly what makes this old townhouse in the trendy Plateau Mont Royal district so cosy and inviting.

belly of Montréal. *Entrance Rue Ste-Catherine*

SPORT & ACTIVITIES

BIXI-BIKES

These bicycles, available on many street corners, offer cheap transport. The basic fee gives you 30 minutes. Payment by credit card: C$5.25/day, C$15/3 days. *montreal.bixi.com*

MONTRÉAL ON WHEELS

Guided bicycle tours through the old town, along the St Lawrence and Lachine Canal. Also bicycle and rollerblade rentals. *Daily 9am–8pm | tel. 877 8 66 06 33 | 27, Rue de la Commune Est | caroulemontreal.com | ▥ e3*

NIGHTLIFE

Experience ballet, theatre and opera in the *Place des Arts (ticket sales tel. 514 8 42 21 12)* performing arts centre. The city's nightlife is concentrated at the mainly English-speaking

Place des Arts

western end of the Rue Ste-Catherine and Rue Crescent. People meet here in the *Sir Winston Churchill (1450, Rue Crescent)*, the *Brutopia* brewery and pub *(1219, Rue Crescent)* or the chic *Wienstein and Gavinos (1434, Rue Crescent)*. In the east the scene revolves around Boulevard St-Laurent and Rue St-Denis.

Popular among the young are the lounge clubs along Boulevard St-Laurent where you can chill out on sofas during the hot summer nights, e.g. *Apt. 200 (3643, Blvd St-Laurent)*, the rooftop terrace of *Don B Comber (3616 Blvd St-Laurent)* or *Blizzarts (3956 A, Blvd St-Laurent)*. Fashionable venues are *L'Amère à Boire (2049, Rue St-Denis)*, *Madame Lee (151, Rue Ontario Est)* and *Café Campus (57, Rue Prince Arthur)* where rock bands frequently perform. Good jazz at *Upstairs (1254, Rue MacKay | upstairsjazz.com)*.

AROUND MONTRÉAL

CHAMBLY
30km / 45 mins by car from Montréal
This small town (pop. 20,000) east of Montréal is a good starting point for the Richelieu River valley tour, for centuries the most important connection from the St Lawrence valley to the south. In the restored 1711 *Fort Chambly* the eventful history of this region – contested by the Iroquois, French, English and Americans – is evident. ▥ *H12*

LAURENTIDES ★
145km / 2 hrs from Montréal
The mountain region of the Laurentides north of the city is the local recreational area for Montréalers. At weekends they come in droves to fish, hike, swim or ski. On weekdays you have the forests almost to yourself. You can find hotels and beautiful bathing lakes around *Sainte-Adèle* and *Sainte-Agathe-des-Monts*. In the 1894 *Parc du Mont-Tremblant* you can go on hikes or bicycle tours and explore over 500 lakes and numerous waterfalls. ▥ *H11*

Laurentides: escape to the country

QUÉBEC

FRANCE IN THE NEW WORLD

Canada's biggest province is unmistakably European in style: pleasantly old-fashioned as well as lively and cosmopolitan. When you follow the St Lawrence east from the Great Lakes you will suddenly find yourself in another world: the road signs now say *Rue* or *Sortie* and no longer *Street* or *Exit*.

You are now in Québec, a province which is a linguistic and cultural bastion of France in British North America. Despite the many

View across to the Pic de L'Aurore at Percé

American influences, the Gallic culture of Québec is very much alive and has even increased in strength over the past 40 years. In old villages, Norman-style houses huddle around big Catholic churches. Montréal displays joie de vivre and a southern European flair, whereas the 400-year-old walled city of Québec evokes a medieval atmosphere.

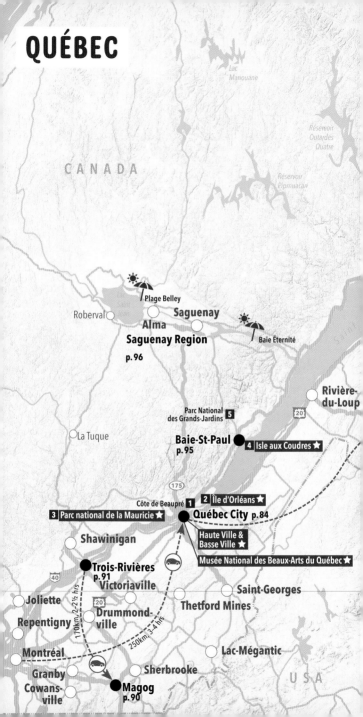

QUÉBEC

CANADA

Lac Manouane

Réservoir Outardes Quatre

Réservoir Pipmuacan

Plage Belley

Saguenay

Roberval

Alma

Saguenay Region
p. 96

Baie Éternité

Rivière-du-Loup

Parc National des Grands-Jardins **5**

La Tuque

Baie-St-Paul
p. 95

4 Isle aux Coudres ★

Côte de Beaupré **1**

2 Île d'Orléans ★

3 Parc national de la Mauricie ★

Québec City p. 84

Haute Ville & Basse Ville ★

Shawinigan

Musée National des Beaux-Arts du Québec ★

Trois-Rivières
p. 91

Victoriaville

Saint-Georges

Joliette

Drummond-ville

Thetford Mines

Repentigny

170km, 2–2½ hrs

250km, 3–4 hrs

Lac-Mégantic

Montréal

Granby

Sherbrooke

USA

Cowans-ville

Magog
p. 90

Sept-Îles

Parc National de
l'Archipel Mingan ★

Mingan-
Archipelag
p. 99

Détroit d'Honguedo

6 Phare de Pointe-des-Monts

● **Baie-Comeau**
p. 97

Ste.-Anne-
des-Monts

Murdochville

Plage Penouille
Plage Haldimand

Parc National Forillon ★

Lawrence River

Matane

Gaspésie
p. 92

Rocher Percé ★

Amqui

Bourg de Pabos

50km, 10 hrs

Campbelton

50 km
31.07 mi

Barthurs

Saint-Quentin

MARCO POLO HIGHLIGHTS

★ **HAUTE VILLE & BASSE VILLE**
Québec's old town with its medieval
buildings is the birthplace of Canada
➤ p. 85

★ **MUSÉE NATIONAL DE
BEAUX-ARTS DU QUÉBEC**
Fine art in the old prison of Québec City
➤ p. 86

★ **ÎLE D'ORLÉANS**
Idyllic villages and wide scenic views of
the St Lawrence ➤ p. 90

★ **PARC NATIONAL DE LA MAURICIE**
The ideal holiday destination for canoeists
and wilderness lovers ➤ p. 92

★ **PARC NATIONAL FORILLON**
Steep cliffs form the last section of the
Gaspésie on the Atlantic ➤ p. 93

★ **ROCHER PERCÉ**
Spectacular sheer rock formation rising
out of the ocean off the Gaspésie ➤ p. 93

★ **ISLE-AUX-COUDRES**
Picture-postcard world of old Québec with
flowering gardens and doll's house
buildings ➤ p. 95

★ **PARC NATIONAL DE
L'ARCHIPEL MINGAN**
The journey to these islands on the
remote north coast of the St Lawrence is
the reward ➤ p. 99

Haute and Basse Ville of Québec City: French flair and lots of history

The St Lawrence River was the most important migration corridor in Canada. The French colonialists settled on the fertile, flat terraces beside the mighty river 350 years ago. Today, about 90 percent of the 8.4 million Québecers live between Montréal and Québec City. Further east, on the Gaspé Peninsula and the northern shore of the 'Saint Laurent', the settlements become more sparse and give way to impressive landscapes of the *belle province*.

The far north of Québec is practically uninhabited. It is a rocky landscape interspersed with lakes, and polished smooth by glaciers, that extends to Hudson Bay and to Ungava Bay on the Arctic Ocean.

The bedrock of the Canadian Shield in this region is the treasure chest of Québec with its large gold, copper and zinc deposits. The southern part of this unspoilt landscape, the densely wooded *Laurentian Mountains*, are easily accessible for tourists: they make ideal bases for extended hikes in summer and skiing in winter.

QUÉBEC CITY

(📖 J11) **The cobblestone alleys, stone city gates and fortified bastions of the old town of Québec City (quebecregion.com) are unique in Canada.**

The provincial capital (pop. 810,000) has a long history. In 2008 the city celebrated the 400th anniversary since its establishment by Samuel de Champlain. Québec has been the French Canadian cultural and economic centre since the 17th century; in 1763 it fell into the hands of the British, but it continues to stay true to the French way of life.

For the most beautiful views of the city, take to the water: a *harbour cruise* is ideal for exploring the old harbour and the wide St Lawrence River. Tip: ☛ It's cheaper to take the ferry to *Lévis* on the south bank (C$3.60 for a single ticket) and the view is just as spectacular *(in summer every 20–30 mins from the old town pier | 10, Rue des Traversiers)*.

The old town is best explored on foot so leave your car in the hotel car park during your visit.

SIGHTSEEING

HAUTE VILLE & BASSE VILLE ★

Basse Ville is located on a narrow waterfront terrace on the St Lawrence where Samuel de Champlain first built a small fortress. Along the Rue de Petit-Champlain and around the Place Royal with the church *Notre-Dame-des-Victoires* (1688) are old buildings with galleries, cafés and souvenir shops. This "lower old town" has been designated a UNESCO Cultural Heritage Site.

Haute Ville is further up on a steep hill and is dominated by the splendid hotel *Le Château Frontenac*. Built in 1924, presidents and kings have slept under its copper roof. All around it are the narrow alleys of the "higher old town" surrounded by the city wall: the lively *Place d'Armes* with *Rue du Trèsor*, where artists display their work Montmartre style; the viewing promenade *Terrasse Dufferin* and the *Rue St-Louis* with its many 17th-century houses. ⎙ *k–m 1–3*

CATHÉDRALE NOTRE-DAME

The 1643 basilica (rebuilt after a fire in 1922) is the oldest parish church in North America. Many pioneers of New France are buried in the crypt. *Daily in summer 7am–7pm, Sun from 8am (guided tours) | 16, Rue Buade | ⎙ l2*

LA CITADELLE

The construction of this star-shaped fortress on the 110-m-high *Cap aux Diamants* took 30 years. The wide

WHERE TO START?

The **Terrasse Dufferin** (⎙ l3) outside the hotel **Le Château Frontenac** is the best place to start. From here you can walk or use the *funiculaire* to get to the old town in Rue de Petit Champlain, Place Royale and the Musée de la Civilisation. Or you can stay in Haute Ville and indulge in a shopping and dining spree on Rue St-Jean.

Parking is available along the river next to the ferry stop (50 Rue Dalhousie) or in the upper town around Grande Allée.

meadows in front of it were the location of the decisive battle between the French and the English in 1759. There are guided tours and a military museum, and in the evening, spooky lantern tours. *Daily in summer 9am–5pm, changing of the guard daily in summer 10am, military tattoo in July/Aug Wed 5pm in the citadel | admission C$16 | entrance from Rue St-Louis | 🗺 l4*

MUSÉE DE LA CIVILISATION

Spectacular building with temporary exhibitions on Québec's cultural history. *Daily in summer 10am–5pm | admission C$17 | 85, Rue Dalhousie | mcq.org | ⏱ 2 hrs | 🗺 m3*

MUSÉE NATIONAL DES BEAUX-ARTS DU QUÉBEC ★

A comprehensive chronology of art in the province: paintings, sculptures and typical craftwork. Also, a new, excellent Inuit art exhibition and a sculpture by David Moore in the old prison tower. *Daily 10am–6pm, Wed until 9pm, in winter until 5pm and closed on Mon | admission C$20 | 179, Grande Allée Ouest | mnba.org | ⏱ 3 hrs | 🗺 J11*

PARC DE L'ARTILLERIE

Exhibition about the city fortifications. Large model of Québec from 1808. *Daily 10am–5pm, closed Oct–March | admission free | 2, Rue d'Auteuil | 🗺 k3*

QUÉBEC CITY

Sagamité
Marché du Vieux-Port
Basse Ville ★
Parc Victoria
Benjo
Noctem
Parc de l'Artillerie
Chez Rioux et Pettigrew
Musée de la Civilisation
Cathédrale Notre-Dame
Le Casse-Crêpe Breton
Le Lapin Sauté
Parc-Bastion de la Reine
La Citadelle
Haute Ville ★
Cosmos Café
Plaines d'Abraham
Musée National des Beaux-Arts du Québec ★

Quai Saint-André
Rue du Prince-Edouard
Rue de la Reine
Rue de la Couronne
Bd. Charest Est
Côte d'Abraham
Av. Honoré-Mercier
Rue Saint-Jean
Rue D'Auteuil
Boulevard Langelier
Rue Signaï
Rue Arago Est
Rue de la Tourelle
Rue Richelieu
Rue Saint-Jean
Bd. René-Lévesque Est
Rue Lockwell
Grande Allée Ouest
Boulevard Champlain
Chemin Sainte-Foy
Avenue De Salaberry
Grande Allée Est
Bd. René-Lévesque Ouest
Avenue des Érables
Rue Aberdeen
Rue Fraser

500 m
547 yd

Musée de la Civilisation: great exhibitions on cultural history and First Nations

EATING & DRINKING

Restaurants often require you to book in advance for lunch. The mostly inexpensive *tables d'hôte* (daily specials) are usually very good.

LE CASSE-CRÊPE BRETON

Affordable and good: generously filled crêpes in a small often-full restaurant. *1136, Rue St-Jean | tel. 418 6 92 04 38 | C$-$$ | Ⅲ k2*

CHEZ RIOUX ET PETTIGREW

Modern cuisine served within old masonry; also traditional regional products such as venison and mushrooms. *1608, Rue St-Paul | tel. 418 6 94 44 48 | C$-$$ | Ⅲ m2*

COSMOS CAFÉ

Popular and pleasant brasserie, excellent for breakfast. *575, Grande Allée Est | tel. 418 6 40 06 06 | C$-$$ | Ⅲ k4*

LE LAPIN SAUTÉ

French country cuisine at reasonable prices in the Basse Ville. With terrace. Beautiful ambience. Specialty: hare. *52, Rue Petit Champlain | tel. 418 6 92 53 25 | C$$ | Ⅲ m3*

NOCTUM

Cool decor, inspired Québec cuisine and designer beers brewed in-house: a great restaurant in the chic district of St Roch on the northern edge of the old town. *438, Rue du Parvis | tel. 581 7 42 79 79 | C$$ | Ⅲ J11*

POUTINE – HOT & GREASY

In English-speaking Canada there are hamburgers, hot dogs and potato chips on every corner, whereas the Québecers are proud of their culinary tradition and haute cuisine, influenced by the Gallic motherland. Yet their secret national dish is *poutine*: a mix of potato chips topped with cheese curds and doused in gravy. In no time at all the crispy, crunchy chips become a peculiar greasy mush. Bon appétit!

SAGAMITÉ

INSIDER TIP
Exquisite First Nation cuisine

Excellent Native American organic restaurant in the hills on the city's edge. Many wild game dishes and regional products. Also, a First Nation museum and an appealing hotel with a natural wood interior. It's worth the journey. *10, Blvd Maurice-Bastien | Wendake | tel. 418 8 47 69 99 | sagamite.com | C$$ | f J11*

SHOPPING

BENJO 😊

The ultimate children's shop with several floors of dolls, model planes, computers, juggling clubs from Cirque du Soleil plus pottery courses and its own children's restaurant. *Mon–Fri 10am–5.30pm, Sat/Sun 9.30am–5pm | 550, Blvd Charest Est | benjo.ca | ⊞ J11*

BOUTIQUE DE NOËL

Year-round Christmas including Santa Claus, Rudolph and bright decorations. *Daily in summer 8am–11pm | 47, Rue de Buade | boutiquedenoel. ca | ⊞ I2*

NIGHTLIFE

The most popular street for an evening stroll is the *Grande Allée* outside the city wall. During the summer the cafés put tables out on the pavement, *chansonniers* strum their guitars and the younger crowd meets up in the bars and cafés. Favourite venues include *Chez Dagobert (600, Grande Allée)* and *Chez Maurice (575, Grande Allée).*

A massive variety of beer awaits you in the *Pub Saint-Alexandre (1087, Rue St-Jean)*.

AROUND QUÉBEC CITY

🔲 CÔTE DE BEAUPRÉ

35km / 45 mins from Québec City

Great for a day trip: Avenue Royale, the "road of the kings" (Route 360), to the northern shore of the St Lawrence, which is steeped in history. The *Bellanger-Girardin House* in Beauport, built in 1673 in the Norman style,

deserves a stop, as do the 83-m-high *Montmorency* waterfalls. Above the falls is the *Manoir Montmorency (tel. 418 6 63 33 30 | C$$)*, a restaurant serving Québecois cuisine with a beautiful view. The history of the region is documented in a visitor centre housed in a 1695 mill in *Château-Richer (7007, Ave Royale)*.

North America's most famous pilgrimage site is *Ste-Anne-de-Beaupré*. In the basement of the Saint Anne basilica – patron saint of sailors – completed in 1923, numerous discarded crutches are evidence of the miracles that have occurred here.

Nearby is a suspension bridge that spans the deep *Canyon Ste-Anne*; at

Rue du Petit-Champlain – one of the many pretty lanes of the Basse Ville

Pilgrimage site: Scala Santa of the Basilica of Ste-Anne-de-Beaupré

Cap Tourmente 300,000 snow geese start their journey to the south in September. Above the river in the *Canyon Ste-Anne (daily 9am–6pm | admission C\$14 | 206, Route 138 Est | Beaupré | tel. 418 8 27 40 57 | canyonsa.qc.ca)* is an adventure playground for the brave with fixed rope routes, rope bridges and several ziplines around a ravine including a 70-m-high waterfall. *J–K11*

2 ÎLE D'ORLÉANS ★

25km / 30 mins from Québec City
Farming villages with picturesque churches are set against the peaceful backdrop of the wide river – as if time has stood still on this 30-km-long island. A circular road provides views of Québec City and the St Lawrence in *Ste-Petronille* and local produce is sold

at road stalls: maple syrup, honey, cider and strawberries. Great stops: the small *Manoir Mauvide-Genest* museum in Saint-Jean and lunch at the *1720 Ancien Moulin (tel. 418 8 29 38 88 | C\$\$)* in Saint-Laurent. *K11*

MAGOG

(J12) **The town (pop. 14,000) on the northern shore of the Lac Memphrémagog lies in the heart of the** *Eastern Townships (eastern townships.org).*

This is the centre of the holiday region with well-maintained hotels, golf courses, lakes and hiking trails in the forested foothills of the

Appalachian Mountains that stretch across the nearby US border to Québec. In *Mont Orford* you can taste the delicious cheese made by monks in the Benedictine abbey of *St-Benoît-du-Lac* and admire the 1920s villas of rich American summer visitors in *North Hatley*.

Worthy of a detour is the small town of *Coaticook* and the *Parc de la Gorge de Coaticook* with a 170-m-high pedestrian bridge over the gorge.

TROIS-RIVIÈRES

(□ J11) **The old industrial city (pop. 160,000) west of Québec City, is primarily a starting point for trips into the St-Maurice Valley.**

On the St Maurice River large quantities of wood are still floated downriver from the hinterland. The old town of the fur-trading post, established in 1634, has many 18th-century houses around the picturesque town hall square and the Rue des Ursulines.

Longest pedestrian bridge in North America over the Gorde de la Coaticook

Ice Age glaciers created countless lakes in the Parc National de la Mauricie

FORGES DU SAINT-MAURICE
The informative industrial museum shows the oldest ironworks in Canada, dating back to 1730. *Daily in summer 10am–5pm | admission C$4 | 10,000, Blvd des Forges*

AROUND TROIS-RIVIÈRES

ⓑ PARC NATIONAL DE LA MAURICIE ★
65km / 1 hr from Trois-Rivières
The national park with many lakes and forests north-west of the city protects the typical landscape of the Canadian Shield and is great for canoeists wanting to make day (or longer) trips *(rental at the info centres at park entrances)*. The St-Maurice Valley on the eastern edge of the park – with hotels and golf courses – is also suitable for hiking. ⌖ *H–J11*

GASPÉSIE

(⌖ L–M 9–10) **With deeply cut coastline, lighthouses and mountain trails, the 300-km-long peninsula extends into the Gulf of St Lawrence and has some of most the impressive landscapes in Québec *(tourismegaspesie.com)*, especially in autumn.**

of the *Chic Choc Mountains*, which is characterised by subarctic vegetation and is one of the oldest mountain ranges in North America, is also home to the *Parc National de la Gaspésie (Route 299)* with 800km² of habitat for moose, bears and caribou.

In the *Parc National Forillon*, on the eastern tip of the Gaspésie Peninsula, the mountains cliffs meet the sea, whereas the southern coast of the park has numerous beaches, such as the long *Plage Penouille*.

In *Gaspé (⌸ N9)* (pop. 15,000), the main town on the peninsula with its long sandy *Plage Haldimand*, a monument on Hwy 132 commemorates the discovery of the region by Jacques Cartier. Route 132 takes you south through the beautiful artist and fishing village of *Percé*.

The *Baie des Chaleurs* on the south coast, surprisingly warm during the summer, is lovely and less rugged. Here you find beautiful holiday resorts, such as *Bonaventure*, with hiking trails and salmon rivers as well as sandy beaches like *Bourg de Pabos* with its surprisingly warm water.

SIGHTSEEING

GASPÉSIE ROUND TRIP

From Québec City, Route 132 takes you through picturesque farming villages on the south bank of the St Lawrence to *Montmagny (⌸ K11)*. Offshore, on the *Île aux Grues*, thousands of snow geese stop off in late summer on their way south (boat tours). *St-Jean-Port-Joli (⌸ K11)* is famous for its woodcarvers. The *Musée des Anciens Canadiens (May–Oct 8.30am–8pm | admission C$8 | on Hwy 132)* highlights works by the Bourgault brothers.

Lighthouses, old villages and long beaches line the way to the east. After *Matane (⌸ L9)* the coasts becomes lonelier and the mountains get closer to the widening river. The hinterland

PARC NATIONAL FORILLON ★

On the north coast, 200-m-high sandstone cliffs tower above the waves of the Atlantic. There are well-maintained hiking trails in the woods along the coast. ⌸ N9

ROCHER PERCÉ ★

The 90-m-high, reddish rock formation is the symbol of the peninsula. Protruding from the surf, it lies off the coast near the village of *Percé*. At low tide you can walk across a sandbank to spot fossils from the Devonian Period embedded in the shale rock. 📖 N10

PARC NATIONAL DE MIGUASHA

The fossils in these cliffs are 380 million years old and include the most beautiful fossil fish in the world, which explains why the park has been declared a UNESCO World Heritage Site. *Daily in summer 9am–5pm | admission C$18 | Nouvelle |* 📖 *M10*

JARDIN DE MÉTIS

INSIDER TIP
Art in the garden

A wonderful garden that is transformed every summer by designers who come from all over the world for an international garden festival. The old mansion houses art galleries and a museum of settler history. *Daily in summer 8.30am–6pm, July/Aug until 8pm | admission C$22 | Route 132 Grand-Métis, between Rimouski and Matane | jardinsdemetis.com | ⊙ 3 hrs |* 📖 *L10*

ÎLE BONAVENTURE

The uninhabited island is a refuge for 30,000 breeding pairs of gannets and other bird species. Boat trips to the bird cliffs and a ferry service for hikers are available. Exhibitions in the *Centre de Découverte Le Chafaud (4, Rue du Quay | Percé | tel. 418 7 82 22 40).*

LA SOCIÉTÉ DUVETNOR

Boat trips go to the islands in the lower St Lawrence region, birdwatching, on request with overnight accommodation in a lighthouse or on a remote island. *Rivière-du-Loup | tel. 418 8 67 16 60 | duvetnor.com*

INSIDER TIP
Just you and the sound of the sea

The Île Bonaventure is a bird refuge – humans have to stay behind fencing

SPORT & ACTIVITIES

ESKAMER ADVENTURE

A few hours or the whole day: kayak trips along the St Lawrence coast. Also canoeing in hinterland canyons. *292 Blvd Perron Est | Ste-Anne-des-Monts | tel. 418 9 67 29 99 | eskamer.ca*

BAIE-ST-PAUL

(⬜ K10) **The small town (pop. 7,300, tourisme-charlevoix.com) in the hills on the northern shore of the St Lawrence has been drawing summer visitors for more than a century.**

Here, the granite massif of the Canadian Shield meets the broad St Lawrence Valley. Dramatic landscapes are guaranteed, especially during the autumn. Many old town buildings house galleries, and sometimes you can visit artists' studios, such as the *Maison René Richard (58, Rue St-Jean-Baptiste)*.

SIGHTSEEING

LE CARREFOUR CULTUREL PAUL-MÉDÉRIC

Exhibition space for paintings, installations and art events. *In summer Tue–Sun 10am–5pm | admission free | 4, Rue Ambroise-Fafard*

MUSÉE D'ART CONTEMPORAIN

Modern building housing temporary exhibitions of regional art. *Daily in summer 10am–5pm | admission C$10 | 23, Rue Ambroise-Fafard | macbsp.com*

EATING & DRINKING

LE BERCAIL

Guy Laliberté, a founder of the Cirque du Soleil, built the ultra-modern resort hotel *Le Germain* in his home town; it has many works of art and a superb restaurant. *50, Rue de la Ferme | tel. 418 2 40 41 00 | legermainhotels.com | C$$*

MOUTON NOIR

Inspired French-Canadian cuisine on a beautiful terrace by the river. *43, Rue Ste-Anne | tel. 418 2 40 30 30 | C$-$$*

AROUND BAIE-ST-PAUL

4 ÎLES AUX COUDRES ★

30km / 1 hr from Baie-St-Paul

A 🚢 free car ferry runs from *St-Joseph-de-la-Rive* to the 16-km-long island with old mills and picturesque villages. ⬜ K10–11

5 PARC NATIONAL DES GRANDS-JARDINS

30km / 30 mins from Baie-St-Paul

This park, set in the bare hilltops of the Laurentides, inland from Baie-St-Paul, is a UNESCO biosphere reserve. Its expanse includes unusual subarctic vegetation, a remnant of the last ice age: meadows filled with white

Colourful autumn leaves transform the landscape around Baie-St-Paul

reindeer moss and small woods of miniature pines reminiscent of the Taiga forest. Highly recommended is the four-hour hiking trail to *Mont du Lac-des-Cygnes*, with magnificent panoramic views of the ancient meteorite crater which formed the region *(access via Route 381 | info centre, exhibitions, hiking trails and camping).*

Immediately to the north, where the Rivière Malbaie has carved out a spectacular 500-m-deep canyon in the granite of the Canadian Shield, is the *Parc National des Hautes-Gorges-de-la-Rivière-Malbaie* with a pristine natural landscape which you can also explore in a canoe. *Access via Route 138 | info for both parks tel. 418 4 39 12 27 | canoe hire and camping | sepaq.com | ▥ K10*

SAGUENAY REGION

(▥ J–K10) **The Saguenay River flows from Lac Saint-Jean to the St Lawrence in a deep fjord valley cut by glaciers.**

In summer, beluga and blue whales gather near the river mouth at *Tadoussac* and can be seen on ferry trips across the bay or special whale-watching tours. Saguenay day cruises from Tadoussac La Baie are organised by *Navettes du Fjord (tel. 418 5 43 76 30 | navettesdufjord.com).*

In the 300-km² *Parc du Saguenay*, steep cliffs tower around the wide ⁂ *Baie Éternité*. There are wonderful hiking trails with fantastic vantage points. At the upper end of the fjord, the commercial port of *Chicoutimi* was one of Québec's early industrial towns. In 1920, the world's biggest wood pulp factory was operated here.

The origin of the Saguenay, *Lac Saint-Jean*, is an almost perfectly round lake from the last ice age with an area of 1,300km². It is a popular sailing and holiday destination with beautiful beaches, such as *Plage Belley* on its northern shore. In summer, blueberries ripen in the forest around the lake which find their way into the region's delicious and well-known blueberry pie.

SIGHTSEEING

CIMM

Large exhibition centre of a whale research organisation; film screenings and boat trips to the belugas at Saguenay. *Daily in summer 9am–8pm | admission C$14, children free | 3-hr boat tours C$70 with croisieresaml. com | at Tadoussac harbour | gremm. org | ⚏ K10*

DER TIP
Dark water, white whales

LA PULPERIE

Fascinating industrial museum in a former wood pulp factory. Also theatre performances. *Daily in summer 9am–6pm | admission C$14.50 | 300, Rue Dubuc | Chicoutimi | pulperie. com | ⚏ K10*

VAL JALBERT

The former industrial town on the shore of Lac Saint-Jean is an open-air

museum. Behind the sawmill is a 72-m-high waterfall. Restaurant, cabins and rooms to rent. *Daily in summer 9am–6pm | admission C$29 | valjalbert.com | ⏱ 3 hrs | ⚏ J10*

ZOO SAUVAGE DE ST-FÉLICIEN

A naturalised park for wild animals with many Canadian species. *Daily in summer 9am–7pm | admission C$42, children C$30 | 2230, Blvd du Jardin | St-Félicien | zoosauvage.org | ⚏ J10*

EATING & DRINKING

CHEZ MARIO TREMBLAY

Restaurant owned by a legendary hockey player. Burgers, salads, steaks. *Rue Collard Ouest | Alma | tel. 418 6 68 72 31 | C$ | ⚏ J10*

LA VOIE MALTÉE

Brewery and pub with innovative beer dishes, terrace, often music at weekends. *777, Blvd Talbot | Chicoutimi | tel. 418 5 49 41 41 | C$-$$ | ⚏ K10*

BAIE-COMEAU

(⚏ L9) **The attractions of this small harbour town (pop. 23,000, *tourismecote-nord.com*) on the secluded north shore of the St Lawrence lie deep in its forested hinterland: seven massive hydro-electric dams retain the Maniconagan and Outardes rivers.**

Mingan Archipelago National Park: sculpture-like rock formations

Dams *Manic 2* and *Manic 5* may be viewed by the public. A ferry connects Baie-Comeau with *Matane* on the southern shore of the St Lawrence, thereby enabling a round trip along both shores of the river.

AROUND BAIE-COMEAU

SIGHTSEEING

JARDIN DES GLACIERS 🐵

An adventure park on the eastern edge of town with high-tech multi-media shows about the last ice age and current global warming. *Daily in summer 8am–5pm | admission C$25–35, children C$16–25 | 3, Ave Denonville | lejardindesglaciers. com*

6 PHARE DE POINTE-DES-MONTS

100km / 1 hr from Baie-Comeau

East of the town a promontory reaches far into the St Lawrence where a lighthouse has guided sailors since 1830; their story is told in the *museum (mid June–early Sept | admission C$12 | pointe-des-monts.com)*. With panoramic terrace and accommodation. The densely wooded granite

IDER TIP

Experience nique nature

shore around the lighthouse creates a unique ecosystem where river and sea meet: ideal for whale- and birdwatching. ▭ *L9*

MINGAN ARCHIPELAGO

(▭ *N8*) **Jacques Cartier's route from Québec City along the northern shore of the St Lawrence ends after 650km in Havre Saint Pierre where you can enjoy boat tours to the islands of the ★** *Parc National de l'Archipel Mingan.*The tides have eroded the soft limestone into bizarre rock columns.

On the long chain of 40 islands off the coast you can view bird colonies and even whales in the salty waters. In *Longue-Pointe* the *Centre d'Interprétation (daily in summer 9am–5pm | admission C$10 | rorqual.com)* provides details about the whales. Book a day in advance to join whale researchers from the *Mingan Island Cetacean Study (MICS) (cost C$2,000 | tel. 418 9 49 28 45)* on an ▐ observation day trip. Boat companies offer half-day tours from Havre-Saint-Pierre to beautiful rock formations *(ticket prices from C$70 | parkscanada.ca).*

WHERE TO STAY IN QUÉBEC

EXPERIENCE NATURE
Ravage means moose pasture, and the eco-wilderness lodge *Auberge du Ravage (12 rooms | 156, Saint-Urbain | Pourvoire de Lac-Moreau | tel. 418 6 65 44 00 | lacmoreau. com | half or full board C$$-$$$)* is true to its name. Good for canoeing and hiking.

HISTORIC
Postmodern meets colonialism: *Hotel Le Priori (15, Rue Sault-au-Matelot | tel. 418 6 92 39 92 | hotellepriori.com | C$$-$$$)* is a designer hotel in a 1766 vicarage with 26 rooms and a superb location in the old town of Québec City.

ATLANTIC COAST

BARREN LAND, RICH SEAS

The wild North Atlantic dominates life in the three mainland provinces on the ocean. Silent mudflats and dramatic fjord coasts are reminiscent of the beautiful landscapes of Scotland or Norway.

In the province of Nova Scotia there are old harbour towns, vineyards and the famous Cabot Trail above the cliffs of Cape Breton Island. The tiny island province of Prince Edward Island, connected to the mainland by a gigantic bridge, creates a very different

Halifax

impression: it's a pastoral landscape with picture-perfect villages and white sandy beaches.

New Brunswick, the heavily forested province, is famous for the highest tidal range in the world. The seabed dries up for miles during low tide – ideal for a walk. And the sea provides food: restaurants in the harbour villages serve freshly caught lobster, Atlantic salmon and exquisite oysters at moderate prices.

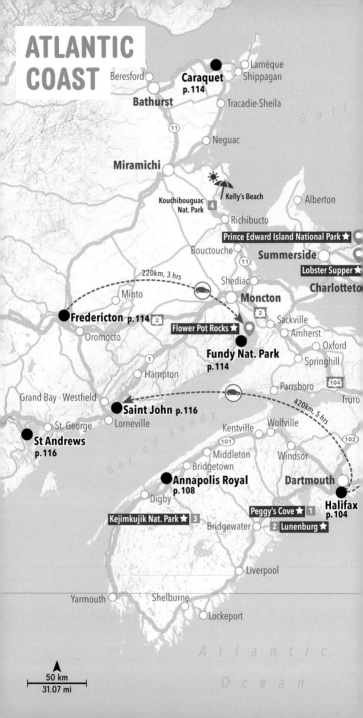

ATLANTIC COAST

Beresford

Caraquet
p. 114

Lamèque
Shippagan

Bathurst

Tracadie-Sheila

(11)

Neguac

Miramichi

Kouchibouguac
Nat. Park 4 Kelly's Beach

Alberton

Richibucto

Prince Edward Island National Park ★

Bouctouche

Summerside

(11)

Lobster Supper ★

Shediac

Charlotteto

220km, 3 hrs

Minto

Moncton

Fredericton p. 114

(2)

(2)

Sackville

Oromocto

Flower Pot Rocks ★

Amherst

Oxford

Fundy Nat. Park
p. 114

Springhill

(1)

Hampton

Parrsboro

(104)

Grand Bay - Westfield

420km, 5 hrs

Truro

Saint John p. 116

Lorneville

(102)

St. George

Kentville

Wolfville

St Andrews
p. 116

(101)

Middleton

Windsor

Bridgetown

Annapolis Royal
p. 108

Dartmouth

Digby

Peggy's Cove ★ 1

Halifax
p. 104

Kejimkujik Nat. Park ★ 3

Bridgewater 2 **Lunenburg** ★

Liverpool

Yarmouth

Shelburne

Lockeport

Atlantic

Ocean

50 km
31.07 mi

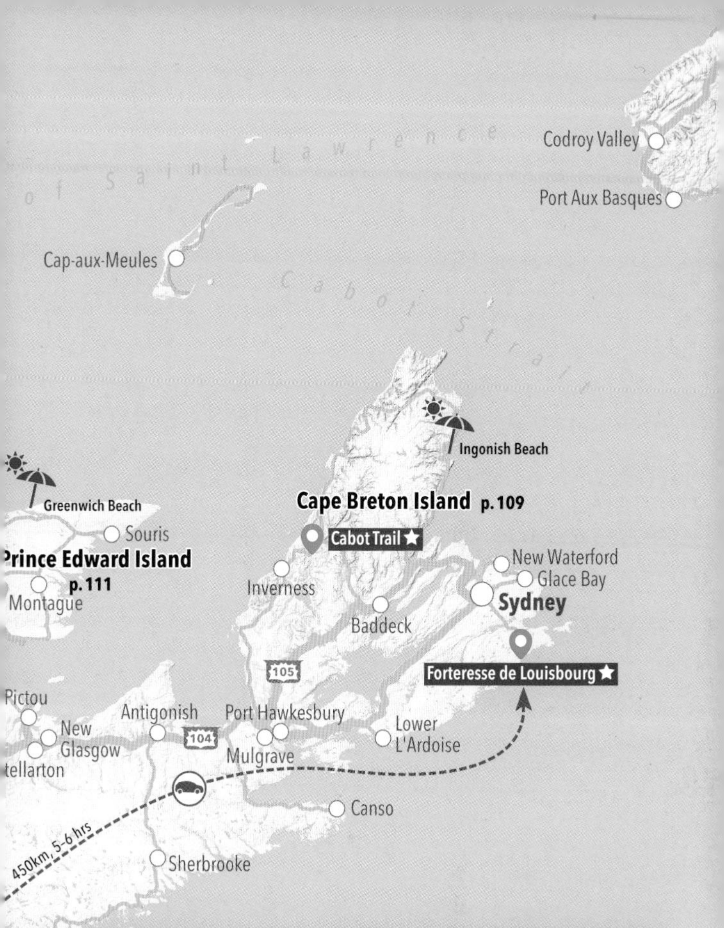

Codroy Valley

Port Aux Basques

Cap-aux-Meules

Gulf of Saint Lawrence

Cabot Strait

Greenwich Beach

Cape Breton Island p. 109

Souris

Cabot Trail ★

Prince Edward Island
p. 111

Ingonish Beach

Montague

Inverness

New Waterford
Glace Bay
Sydney

Baddeck

[105]

Pictou

Antigonish
[104]

Port Hawkesbury

Forteresse de Louisbourg ★

New
Glasgow

Mulgrave

Lower
L'Ardoise

Stellarton

Canso

450km, 5–6 hrs

Sherbrooke

MARCO POLO HIGHLIGHTS

★ **PEGGY'S COVE**
Selfie spot: a white lighthouse on the cliffs
near Halifax ➤ p. 107

★ **LUNENBURG**
Historic harbour town with charm and
steep streets ➤ p. 107

★ **KEJIMKUJIK NATIONAL PARK**
Follow the early fur traders and take a
canoe trip ➤ p. 108

★ **CABOT TRAIL**
The most beautiful scenic road on the
Atlantic is a dream during the 'Indian
Summer' ➤ p. 109

★ **FORTERESSE DE LOUISBOURG**
A new life for France's fortress in the New
World ➤ p. 110

★ **LOBSTER SUPPER**
Delicious seafood on Prince Edward Island
➤ p. 112

★ **PRINCE EDWARD ISLAND**
NATIONAL PARK
Red sandy beaches, wide dunes and so
much space ➤ p. 113

★ **FLOWER POT ROCKS**
A unique natural phenomenon formed by
the tides ➤ p. 114

Historic sailing ships frequently moor in the harbour of the Maritime Museum

HALIFAX

(*N12*) **The capital of Nova Scotia (pop. 425,000, *novascotia.com*) is not only the economic and cultural centre of this province, but also of the whole Canadian Atlantic region.**

Halifax is a hard-working port city – as you can see from the many merchant and naval ships – with a natural harbour over 25km long.

Students from five universities help give Halifax its youthful image, and on Friday and Saturday the city has an active nightlife.

At the same time, Halifax is proud of its history. In 1749 the English chose the ice-free, strategically situated bay as a base and established a fort on the steep hill overlooking the harbour. Under the protection of the citadel, which emerged from this fort, Halifax blossomed into a rich trading town. Not a single shot was ever fired from the fortress, but Atlantic convoys left from here for England during both world wars.

SIGHTSEEING

CITY CENTRE

The historic centre of the city is the *Grand Parade*, a small park flanked by the town hall and *St Paul's Church*, the oldest Anglican Church in Canada, built in 1750. Further down the hill the elegant *Province House*, built in Georgian style in 1818, is now Nova Scotia's Parliament.

HALIFAX CITADEL
The fortress was built between 1828 and 1856 in a commanding position overlooking the city. It now houses a military museum and its four-sided town clock is a Halifax landmark. *In summer 9am–6pm, otherwise until 5pm | admission C$12, low season C$8*

HARBOURFRONT
The warehouses and piers along the Lower Water Street once belonged to *privateers*, the king's pirates who stowed their booty here. Today, boutiques and bars line the attractively restored waterfront district. Especially successful is the *Historic Properties* complex with its narrow lanes and 19th-century warehouses.

MARITIME MUSEUM 🛶
You can discover interesting facts about sailing and steamships in the North Atlantic, but most visitors come to see relics from the *Titanic*, including an original deck chair. The Fairview Lawn Cemetery is the last resting place of many who died in the tragedy. *Daily 9.30am–5.30pm, Tue until 8pm, otherwise Tue–Sat 9.30am–5pm, Sun 1pm–5pm | admission C$9.55 | 1675 Lower Water St | maritimemuseum. novascotia.ca*

DISCOVERY CENTRE 👥
Engineering, technology, hands-on experiments and a real bush aircraft.

Daily 10am–5pm, Wed until 8pm | admission C$12, children C$10 | 1593 Barrington St | thediscoverycentre.ca

PIER 21 – CANADA'S IMMIGRATION MUSEUM
Fascinating museum telling the story of one million immigrants who arrived from Europe between 1928 and 1971. *Daily in summer 9.30am–5.30pm, otherwise Tue–Sat 10am–5pm | admission C$14.50 | 1055 Marginal Rd | pier21.ca | ⏱ 2 hrs*

EATING & DRINKING

MCKELVIE'S
Popular seafood restaurant in an old fire station. *1680 Lower Water St | tel. 902 4 21 61 61 | C$$*

SALTY'S ON THE WATERFRONT
Good choice for salmon and lobster: the upper floor offers fine dining with a harbour view, while the ground floor

---

WHERE TO START?
The waterfront – naturally. From there, take a stroll around the **Historic Properties** and visit the Maritime Museum with its Titanic exhibition. From here it is only 400m uphill to George Street and the Grand Parade park, and another 900m to the town clock at the Halifax Citadel.

Park at the bottom of George Street and at the southern end of the harbour (also for motorhomes). Several buses stop at Water Street.

has pub seafood on the terrace. *Historic Properties | 1877 Upper Water St | tel. 902 4 23 68 18 | C\$\$–\$\$\$*

SPLIT CROW 🚩

Rustic bar in the old town, often live music in the evenings. To see who is playing visit *splitcrow.com*. *1855 Granville St | tel. 902 4 22 43 66 | C\$*

THE WOODEN MONKEY

Only regional, organic products are used in the dishes of this popular restaurant in the old town. Delicious blueberry and apple turnover with maple syrup. *1707 Grafton St | tel. 902 4 44 38 44 | C\$-\$\$*

SHOPPING

Galleries, souvenirs, First Nation crafts and nautical bric-à-brac can be found in the *Historic Properties*. Shopping malls and boutiques are situated on *Duke Street* and *Spring Garden Road*.

Arts and crafts made in Nova Scotia are in the *Centre for Craft and Design (1061 and 1096 Marginal Rd)*. The *Seaport farmer's market (closed Mon | Marginal Rd)* in the cruise ship harbour has artworks as well as jams, smoked fish and other regional products.

Seafaring meets café culture at the Fisheries Museum of the Atlantic in Lunenburg

SPORT & ACTIVITIES

COASTAL ADVENTURES
Kayak tours along the east coast of Nova Scotia. Also kayak rental. *Tangier | tel. 902 7 72 27 74 | coastal adventures.com*

MURPHY'S – THE CABLE WHARF
Harbour sightseeing trips on a paddle steamer or tall ship and entertaining tours on the amphibious "Harbour Hopper". *C\$36–75 | Cable Wharf | tel. 902 4 20 10 15 | mtcw.ca*

NIGHTLIFE

Halifax nightlife is concentrated in the bars and clubs around *Argyle Street* and *Grafton Street* near the Grand Parade. There's popular live music at the *Carlton (1685 Argyle St)*. The *Dome (1726 Argyle St)* is a complex with multiple dance floors.

AROUND HALIFAX

1 PEGGY'S COVE ★ ⛤
45km / 1 hr by car from Halifax
A lighthouse perched on wave-swept granite rocks with colourful fishermen's cottages: this is Peggy's Cove, south-west of Halifax, with only 60 residents and considered to be the most picturesque fishing harbour on the Atlantic. It gets really busy in summer but is still worth a visit. South of the village is a simple memorial for the victims of the Swissair crash in September 1998. *N12*

2 LUNENBURG ★
100km / 1.5 hrs by car from Halifax
Many of the 2,300 residents of this pretty fishing harbour on the south coast of Nova Scotia are descendants of the Germans and Swiss who settled here around 1750. The *Bluenose* schooner – which won many sailing regattas and adorns the 10 cent coin – was built here in 1921.

The village, a UNESCO World Heritage Site, is characterised by boatyards and beautifully preserved captains' villas.

Seafaring and fishing in the harsh North Atlantic are depicted in the *Fisheries Museum of the Atlantic (daily in summer 9.30am–5.30pm, winter until 5pm | admission C$12 | 68 Bluenose Dr.)*, which has an aquarium and several original fishing boats. *N13*

③ KEJIMKUJIK NATIONAL PARK ★

170km / 2.5 hrs by car from Halifax
The interior of Nova Scotia offers idyllic lakes and rivers – perfect for swimming, camping and canoeing. Canoe rental is available from *Keji Outfitters (tel. 902 6 82 22 82 | whynotadventure. ca)* at Jake's Landing. *N13*

④ KOUCHIBOUGUAC NATIONAL PARK

350km / 3.5 hrs by car from Halifax
Swampy forests, lagoons and magnificent sandy beaches are the attractions of this 240-km² nature reserve on the east coast of New Brunswick.

The park has almost 50km of cycle paths through the dunes (bicycles available at *Ryan's Rental Centre* near the campsite). Half-day tours in large voyageur canoes set out from *Cape St Louis (tel. 506 8 76 24 43)*. A boardwalk by the sea leads to ✵ *Kelly's Beach* which stretches 10km along the Northumberland Strait.

In the south of the park, the French-Canadian village of *Bouctouche*, home to the *Pays de la Sagouine (sagouine. com)* cultural centre, presents theatre performances depicting the harsh living conditions in an Acadian fishing village 100 years ago. *M–N11*

ANNAPOLIS ROYAL

(M12) **Surrounded by picturesque farmlands, this small village (pop. 500) lies on the Bay of Fundy in the north-west of Nova Scotia. There are Victorian houses lining pretty streets, the old British Fort Anne and historic gardens.**

In 1605 Samuel de Champlain founded the *Habitation Port Royal (in summer 9am–5.30pm | admission C$4)*, the first settlement in Canada, on the opposite bank of the *Annapolis Valley*. There are re-enactments at *Fort Anne* with costumed *guides* demonstrating the pioneer life. Markets on Wednesdays and Saturdays sell fruit, vegetables and arts and crafts. The nearby *tidal power plant* makes use of the Bay of Fundy's high tides and has good exhibitions in the *Interpretive Centre (236 Prince Albert Rd)*.

EATING & DRINKING

COMPOSE
Canadian-Austrian cuisine with a marvellous view of the ocean. *235 Saint George St | tel. 902 5 32 12 51 | C$$*

GARRISON HOUSE
Regional food in a historic house with a beautiful conservatory. Try the famous *Digby scallops* from nearby

Digby harbour. The adjoining B&B and inn have 7 rooms. *350 St George St | tel. 902 5 32 57 50 | garrisonhouse.ca | C$$*

CAPE BRETON ISLAND

(□ O-P11) **'Ciad mile failte!' A hundred thousand welcomes!** The old Gaelic greeting is still heard on Cape Breton Island *(cbisland.com).*

For more than 200 years the Scots have settled on this 10,000-km² island whose barren highlands and rugged coastline are reminiscent of the Scottish Highlands.

SIGHTSEEING

BRETON ISLAND ROUND TRIP
An island sightseeing trip full of history and spectacular nature starts at the resort of *Baddeck* in the north of the 70-km-long saltwater *Bras d'Or Lake*. On a day trip you can go from Baddeck on the 300-km ★ ▀ *Cabot Trail* and round the northern tip of the island. It is famous for being the most beautiful scenic road in Eastern Canada: remote cliffs and quiet moorland; red granite rocks that glisten in the spray; and tiny fishing villages with stacks of wooden lobster traps. And if that has whetted your appetite, try the ▀ *Oceanside Chowder Hut.* The three sisters in the small shack at the end of the street in *Meat Cove* are fantastic cooks.

INSIDER TIP
Mussel soup at the end of the world

The prettiest part of the route runs through the *Cape Breton Highlands National Park* (great hiking, such as the 7-km *Skyline Trail*). Near the park's northern entrance you will hear

The Skyline Trail in the highlands of Cape Breton is true to its name

Travel back in time to 1744: Forteresse de Louisbourg

French being spoken. The small *Chéticamp* is an Acadian enclave. Their ancestors, French settlers from Nova Scotia and New Brunswick, fled from the English in 1755 to this inhospitable region. In the *Acadian Museum* and in the various galleries you can admire their traditional craftwork.

Take Hwy 22 on a detour to the rugged south of the island, past coalfields and the port town of *Sydney*, from where the ferry leaves for Newfoundland.

ALEXANDER GRAHAM BELL NATIONAL HISTORIC SITE

This large museum is next to the home of Bell, inventor of the telephone who also did pioneering research on the hydrofoil and on aeronautics. *Summer 9am–5pm | admission C$8 | Baddeck*

FORTERESSE DE LOUISBOURG ★ 👥

Soldiers on parade, haggling fur traders and governing aristocrats – this living museum reproduces life in 1744. Even the two restaurants in this museum town use recipes from the 18th century – and the rum is authentic too. On summer evenings the village serves a *Beggars Banquet*. *Daily 9.30am–5pm | admission C$18, children free | Louisbourg | ⏱ 5 hrs*

GLENORA DISTILLERY

Whiskey fans can taste North America's first single malt. The distillery has an excellent restaurant and a small country inn. *Daily 9am–5pm | food C$7, guided tours | Route 19 | Glenville*

EATING & DRINKING

CHANTERELLE

This restaurant serves excellent regional cuisine using organically grown produce. In summer fresh *chanterelles* from the forest often feature on the menu. The restaurant is part of the comfortable solar-powered *Chanterelle Country Inn* which has 12 rooms and cabins. *48678 Cabot Trail | Baddeck | tel. 866 2 77 05 77 | chanterelleinn.com | C$$-$$$*

KELTIC LODGE

An elegant, historic hotel restaurant with a breathtaking view serving regional specialities such as lobster and Solomon Gundy. 🏃 *Ingonish Beach | tel. 902 2 85 28 80 | kelticlodge.ca | C$$*

RED SHOE PUB

INSIDER TIP
Rhythm and fiddle music

Enjoy the local character: fiddle music plays a major role in this popular pub. There's live music almost every evening as well as good wholesome regional cooking: *redshoepub. com. 11573 Hwy 19 | Mabou | tel. 902 9 45 29 96 | C$-$$*

SPORT & ACTIVITIES

KAYAK CAPE BRETON

Guided kayaking tours on the Bras d'Or Lake and along the coast, in addition to canoe and kayak rental. There are also three log cabins available. *West Bay | tel. 902 5 35 30 60 | kayakcapebreton.com*

WHALE WATCHING

Along the island's north coast there are summer boat trips to bird islands and sea caves, e.g. *Pleasant Bay by Captain Mark's (tel. 902 2 24 13 16 | whaleandsealcruise.com)* or *Neil's Harbour by Dixon's Zodiak Seafari (tel. 855 2 59 41 22 | dixonszodiacseafari. com)*. If you don't see any whales, many operators offer a complimentary trip the next day.

PRINCE EDWARD ISLAND

(📖 N–O11) **Red potato fields, fine sandy beaches and well-kept cottages of the fishermen and farmers are lasting impressions of this green island on the southern edge of the Gulf of St Lawrence** *(tourism pei.com).*

It is Canada's smallest province: 200km long and 60km wide. Due to its bay-lined coast, Prince Edward Island (or *PEI*) has almost 800km of beaches. And because the sea reaches temperatures of over 20°C in summer, it is a popular holiday destination for many Canadians. The fast Northumberland Strait car ferry connects the island to the port of *Pictou* and, since 1998, the 12.9-km *Confederation Bridge* has connected *Cape Tormentine* in New Brunswick to *Borden* on PEI. There are four signposted scenic routes that will take

You can't miss the signs of lobster fishing on Prince Edward Island

you – mostly on idyllic back roads – to all the regions of the island.

The proud claim of PEI is that it has the best lobster in Canada. You can put this to the test in one of the many seafood restaurants or at a traditional ★ *lobster supper*. These are not the elegant, refined evenings you might expect: they are rather loud and rustic – and touristy, too – often served in a community hall or in a shed at the harbour. The menu is usually chowder followed by a large lobster with a coleslaw or macaroni salad, corn on the cob and dessert – nobody goes hungry. The famous Malpeque oysters, which are bred in a shallow bay near *Malpeque*, are also delicious.

ALEXANDER GRAHAM BELL

While the United States has Thomas Edison, Canada has Alexander G Bell (1847–1922). The Scottish-born Bell found fame in Ontario with his invention of the telephone in 1875. His Bell Telephone Company continues his legacy today in the form of telecoms giant AT&T. Bell began his experiments in Nova Scotia in 1886 in the fields of medicine, aviation and marine technology. He developed the iron lung and also worked on special educational methods for the deaf – a personal concern because both his mother and his wife were deaf.

SIGHTSEEING

CHARLOTTETOWN

The capital of the province (pop. 33,000), established by the French in 1720, has preserved its charming small-town atmosphere. In the restored *Old Charlottetown* are a number of magnificent townhouses

Daily in summer 9.30am–5pm | admission C$4 | Hwy 16 | Souris

EATING & DRINKING

THE DUNES
Chic bistro with potter's studio in a modern glass and wood building. They serve regional fish and lamb dishes from organic farms. *Route 15 | Brackley Beach | tel. 902 6 72 25 86 | C$$*

FISHBONE'S SEAFOOD GRILL
Oysters, mussels, lobster, fish – all served in an old townhouse in the heart of Charlottetown. *136 Richmond St | tel. 902 6 28 65 69 | C$-$$*

that were once the homes of wealthy captains and merchants. Lovely for a stroll is *Great George Street* with its restaurants and small shops.

NORTH COAST/CAVENDISH
The most beautiful beaches are in the north: white sandy ones around *Souris*, and reddish sandy ones in the ★ *PEI National Park* at the popular resort town of *Cavendish*. Various bays, dunes and lagoons around the *Greenwich Interpretive Centre* on the seemingly endless *Greenwich Beach* are home to water birds and many migratory birds – more than 300 species have been spotted here.

BASIN HEAD FISHERIES MUSEUM
In a beautiful setting on the coast, this museum has a small aquarium and exhibitions about the fishing industry.

LEONHARD'S
German bread and pastries, great breakfast and lunch – all organic – on the main shopping street in Charlottetown. *Daily 9am–5pm | 142 Great George St | tel. 902 3 67 36 21 | leonhards.ca | C$*

NEW GLASGOW LOBSTER SUPPERS
The whole village helps to serve visitors with an evening of fish soup, mussels and *lobster* – a tradition that goes back 50 years. *Route 258 | New Glasgow | tel. 902 9 64 28 70 | C$$*

SPORT & ACTIVITIES

OUTSIDE EXPEDITIONS
Kayak and cycling tours on the north coast of the island. Also bicycle and paddleboard rental. *370 Harbourview Dr. | North Rustico | tel. 902 9 63 33 66 | getoutside.com*

FUNDY NATIONAL PARK

(M12) **The hilly hinterland of the almost 200-km² park on the south coast of New Brunswick ends at the shore of the Bay of Fundy with its 60-m-high cliffs.**

The funnel-shaped bay has an impressive tidal range – the largest fluctuation in the world. At high tide the water is at 10m, while at low tide you can walk on the dry mud flats (guided tours by park wardens). You can also hike on trails such as the *Coastal Trail* from *Herring Cove* along the forested coast and *Matthews Head* to *Point Wolfe* (7km).

INSIDER TIP
Fantastic sea view

At *Hopewell Cape*, 40km east of the park, the tidal range is particularly evident: at high tide the ★ *Flowerpot Rocks* (as the locals call them) are small islands, but six hours later they tower 15m above the dry seabed.

The ⚑ restaurant in the *Cape D'Or Lighthouse* (*Advocate Harbour | tel. 1 902 6 70 83 14 | capedor.ca | C$-$$*) serves fabulous fish with a great view. The cosy *Captains Inn B&B* is in an old villa close to the park entrance (*8 rooms | Alma | tel. 506 8 87 20 17 | captainsinn.ca | C$*).

CARAQUET

(M10) **The harbour town (pop. 4,100) on the Baie des Chaleurs in the north-east of New Brunswick is the centre of the Péninsule Acadienne, an Acadian settler district. Here, both the language and old French culinary arts are still maintained.**

The *Village Historique Acadien (June–early Sept daily 10am–6pm | admission C$20 | Hwy 11, 10km west of Caraquet | villagehistoriqueacadien. com)* is an extensive museum village that recreates the pioneer life and craft skills of the French settlers. "Acadians" in costume plough the fields, work in the blacksmith's shop and serve in the tavern. You can enjoy Acadian cuisine in an 1891 house – the *Hotel Paulin (143, Blvd St-Pierre Ouest | hotel paulin.com | C$$*).

FREDERICTON

(M11–12) **In the valley of the Saint John River, the capital of New Brunswick (pop. 60,000, *tourism newbrunswick.ca*) has a small-town atmosphere with well-kept gardens and attractive buildings.**

Originally founded by the French, many British loyalists moved here from the United States in 1785. The military buildings on Queen Street (now museums), the neo-Gothic *Christ Church Cathedral* in the city centre and the beautifully situated *University of*

New Brunswick all attest to the influence of the British. On summer evenings the *Historic Garrison District* is good for a stroll, with concerts, street theatre and films.

SIGHTSEEING

BEAVERBROOK ART GALLERY

Excellent art museum with paintings by William Turner and Thomas Gainsborough as well as modern Canadian art. *Tue-Sun 10am-5pm, Thu until 9pm, Sun from noon, winter closed on Mon | admission C$10 | 703 Queen St | beaverbrookartgallery.org*

KINGS LANDING

When a dam was built on the Saint John River, 25 historical buildings were saved from flooding and used to recreate an 18th-century British loyalist village. "Citizen" actors work at looms and serve hearty food in the *King's Head Inn. Early June-early Oct daily 10am-5pm | admission C$18, children C$13.50 | on Hwy 2 | 35km west of Fredericton | kingslanding. nb.ca | ⏱ 4 hrs*

SHOPPING

Saturday mornings are a social affair at the *farmer's market (George St 655).*

The full height of the Flowerpot Rocks only becomes apparent at low tide

Fresh fruit and vegetables in the Old City Market in Saint John

Stalls offer organic vegetables and regional specialities from fern tips and blueberries to falafel and bison burgers.

SAINT JOHN

(*M12*) **New Brunswick's largest city (pop. 126,000), at the mouth of the Saint John River in the Bay of Fundy, has one of Canada's most important Atlantic harbours.**

The small old town at the river mouth has been restored and invites visitors to stroll in the *Old City Market*. The *New Brunswick Museum (Mon–Fri 9am–5pm, Thu until 9pm, Sat 10am–5pm, Sun noon–5pm | admission C$10 | 1 Market Square |* *nbm-mnb.ca)* is the oldest museum in Canada and showcases everything from the geology to the pioneer history of New Brunswick.

The city's biggest attraction is the *Saint John River*, where tides cause the river to reverse its flow twice a day – at high tide the sea water pushes inland. The phenomenon can be seen (possibly from a zipline) at the *Reversing Rapids (visitor centre).*

SAINT ANDREWS

(*M12*) **The peaceful harbour village (pop. 1,900) on Passamaquoddy Bay is only a** stone's throw away from the US State of Maine.

For more than 100 years it has been a popular summer holiday destination with beautiful golf courses and beaches. Picturesque old wooden houses line *Water Street*, which features small shops and seafood restaurants. The Roaring Twenties are alive and well in Saint Andrews-by-the-Sea: the *Algonquin Resort (184 Adolphus St)* is an exquisite hotel with a large veranda, golf course and extensive gardens.

Saint Andrews is also a good base for whale-watching tours or trips to Deer Island, Campobello Island and Grand Manan Island.

IDER TIP
Pose like atsby on the veranda

Saint Andrews, New Brunswick

NEWFOUNDLAND & LABRADOR

This remote region of Eastern Canada is in a different time zone – half an hour ahead of Atlantic Time – a peculiarity that fits in with the different feel of the land and its people.

Just 500,000 people live on the island (about 100,000km²), with its magnificent fjord landscape, and they call their home "the rock". A thousand years ago the Vikings established a settlement at the northern tip of the current Newfoundland. Later, shortly after

Icebergs off the rocky coast of Newfoundland

Columbus, John Cabot paved the way for the English, French, Basque and Portuguese who followed. Newfoundland only became a province of the State of Canada in 1949.

Labrador is the mainland part of the province. It's a wild, almost completely unexplored world of lonely fjords and bays filled with icebergs – but also with legendary ore deposits, as demonstrated by the trove of nickel that was discovered in Voisey Bay in 1993.

NEWFOUNDLAND & LABRADOR

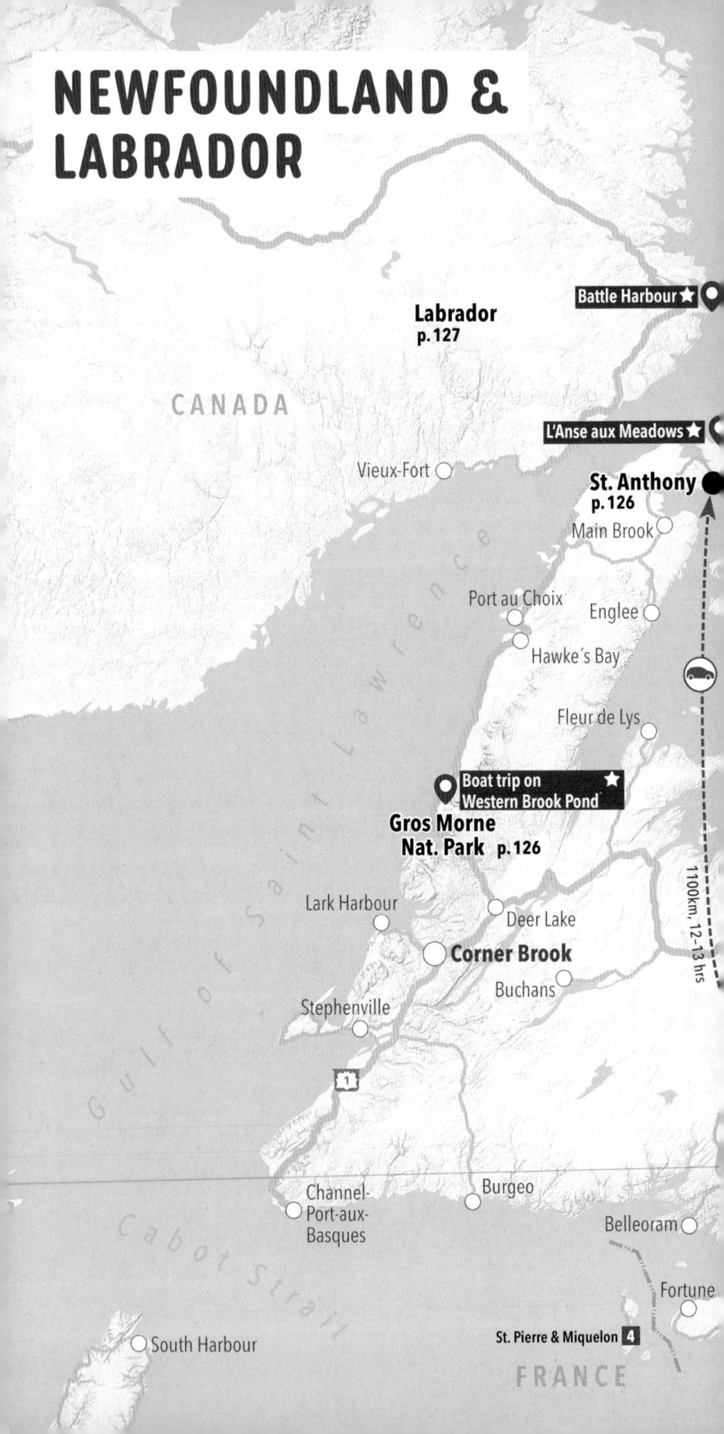

Labrador
p. 127

CANADA

Battle Harbour ★

L'Anse aux Meadows ★

St. Anthony ●
p. 126

Vieux-Fort ○

Main Brook ○

Port au Choix ○

Englee ○

Hawke's Bay ○

Fleur de Lys ○

Boat trip on Western Brook Pond ★

Gros Morne Nat. Park p. 126

Lark Harbour ○

Deer Lake ○

Corner Brook ○

Buchans ○

Stephenville ○

1100 km, 12–13 hrs

Gulf of Saint Lawrence

1

Channel-Port-aux-Basques ○

Burgeo ○

Belleoram ○

Fortune ○

Cabot Strait

South Harbour ○

St. Pierre & Miquelon 4

FRANCE

Twillingate ★ p. 125

Atlantic

Ocean

445km, 6 hrs

1

○ Bonavista

Glovertown ○

Old Perlican ○

Goobies ○

St John's p. 122 ● **1** Cape Spear

1

Placentia ○

175km, 3-4 hrs

2 Colony of Avalon

3 Cape St Mary's ★

100 km
62.14 mi

ST JOHN'S

The capital of the province of Newfoundland & Labrador (pop. 210,000, *newfoundlandlabrador. com*) is one of the oldest cities in North America. It lies in a protected bay on the southeast coast of the island. Its lively centre is Duckworth Street above the harbour.

In the 17th century, the English and the French, who had come to fish for cod, fought over the year-round ice-free, natural harbour. For the past four centuries the people of Newfoundland have been living from cod fishing on the Grand Banks – a mainland shelf protruding far into the Atlantic with a once-legendary abundance of fish. John Cabot himself wrote that you "only had to lower a bucket into the sea to lift it out full of fish". However, decades of overfishing resulted in a dramatic fall in numbers so that, in the 1990s, many fishermen lost their jobs. Only now are stocks slowly recovering.

Today big vessels moored here in the harbour tell of renewed hope for the economy: they supply the oil rigs off the east coast of the island. *S9*

SIGHTSEEING

THE ROOMS

This excellent provincial museum has exhibitions on pioneer history and the region's art and culture. The café serves reasonably priced salads and typical Newfoundland food for lunch. Delicious fish chowder. *Summer Mon–Sat 10am–5pm, Wed until 9pm, Sun noon–5pm | admission C$10 | 9 Bonaventure Av. | therooms.ca*

ST JOHN THE BAPTIST

The Catholic cathedral, built in 1841, has a richly decorated interior. *Daily 8am–4pm, Sat until 5pm, Sun 8am–12.30pm | admission free| Military Rd*

NEWFIES

The Newfoundlanders' accent and lifestyle often make them the target of jokes in other parts of Canada. But the Newfies have a sense of humour and bear their fate in a laid-back manner. A collection of typical jokes and more information about the island can be found at *upalong.org*.

Vast land: Signal Hill has the best scenic views of St John's

ST JOHN THE BAPTIST

The Anglican cathedral (1849) bears the same name as the Catholic one. In July/August afternoon tea and scones are served (Wed–Sat) in the *Krypta Tearoom (C$10). Daily in summer 10am–4pm, Sat until noon | admission free | 16 Church Hill*

CABOT TOWER/SIGNAL HILL

The first radio contact with Europe was made in 1901 from the tower that overlooks the harbour. Best views are from the 160-m-high *Signal Hill*, especially in the morning. *Exhibitions inside. Daily in summer 10am–6pm | admission C$4*

JOHNSON GEO CENTRE 👯

The mostly underground science museum explains the fascinating geology of Newfoundland. There is also a special exhibition on the tragic fate of the *Titanic*, that sank only 500km from here in the North Atlantic. *Daily 9.30am–5pm, winter closed on Mon | admission C$12, children C$6 | 175 Signal Hill Rd | geocentre.ca | ⏱ 1 hr*

> **INSIDER TIP**
> **The doomed Titanic**

FLUVARIUM 👯

Interesting ecological exhibitions with a stream that is viewed through underwater windows. *Summer Mon–Fri 9am–5pm, Sat/Sun from 10am | admission C$8, children C$6 | Pippy Park | ⏱ 1 hr*

EAST COAST TRAIL

Spectacular 220-km trail along the east coast of the Avalon Peninsula south from St John's *(eastcoasttrail.com)*. Some legs feature rope bridges and boardwalks. Tours with accommodation and baggage transport are offered by *Trail Connections (tel. 709 3 35 83 15 | trailconnections.ca).*

O'BRIENS BOAT TOURS

This place offers boat trips to the bird rocks and for whale watching off Newfoundland's eastern cape. *Bay Bulls | 2–3-hr tour C$65 | tel. 709 7 53 48 50 | obriensboattours.com*

EATING & DRINKING

CLASSIC CAFÉ EAST

Hearty Newfoundland food and excellent breakfast. You can sit out on the terrace in good weather. *73 Duckworth St | tel. 709 7 26 44 44 | C$-$$*

TRAPPER JOHN'S

Historically styled pub, famous for its *screech-in* ceremony where visitors are sworn in by kissing a cod (or a stuffed puffin) and then downing a shot of rum. *2 George St | tel. 709 5 79 96 30 | C$*

SHOPPING

In the shops along *Water Street* and *Duckworth Street* you will find nautical souvenirs, traditional knitted gloves and arts and crafts from remote villages.

AROUND ST JOHN'S

1 CAPE SPEAR

10km / 30 mins by car from St John's
This windblown headland south-east of St John's has a 19th-century lighthouse and is the easternmost point of North America. Beautiful at sunrise provided there is no fog. *S9*

INSIDER TIP
Be the first to see the sunrise

2 COLONY OF AVALON

75km / 1–2 hrs by car from St John's
Ferryland has excavations of the oldest English settlement in Newfoundland – established in 1621. Join the archaeologists at work and see exhibitions on its riveting history. *colonyofavalon.ca | S10*

3 CAPE ST MARY'S ★ 🎭

150km / 3 hrs by car from St John's
In summer, huge colonies of gannets and gulls gather on the rocky headland in the south-west of the Avalon Peninsula. A high vantage point provides a good view of the colonies. *S10*

4 ST PIERRE & MIQUELON

350km / 6–7 hrs by car and ferry from St John's
These two small islands off the south coast of Newfoundland have been a French enclave since colonial times. The islanders speak French and you pay in euros. There are beaches, the rocky coastline and seal colonies. *saint pierreferry.ca | R10*

INSIDER TIP
EU in Canada

TWILLINGATE

A labyrinth of islands and bays surrounds the fishing village of ★ Twillingate (pop. 2,600) on Newfoundland's north coast, although its main attraction is "Iceberg Alley".

Just off the coast near Twillingate, mighty blocks of ice drift down from the Arctic carried south by the Labrador Current. From April until early July you can view these massive, bizarrely shaped, glittering giants from boat tours and from the *Long Point Lighthouse*. For satellite infomation on up-to-date iceberg locations, visit *icebergfinder.com*.

Worth a visit is the island of *Fogo* (car ferry) which has a great fishing museum and an art project with architecturally impressive studios for international artists *(shorefast. org)*. ⏛ *R8*

SIGHTSEEING

TWILLINGATE ADVENTURE TOURS

Two-hour boat trip to see icebergs, whales and sea lions in Notre Dame Bay. *Tel. 709 8 84 59 99 | twillin gateadventuretours.com*

In the past, life here was all about fishing, but today Twillingate depends on tourism

history. A ⭐ *boat trip on the Western Brook Pond (tel. 709 4 58 20 16 | bontours.ca)*, a 15-km inland fjord, takes you past 600-m cliffs. A 45-minute walk leads to the lake where moose are often spotted. Other boat trips are available to *Bonne Bay* and the beautiful *Bay of Islands*, further south. 📖 *Q8*

ST ANTHONY

The legendary Viking colony of *Vinland* actually existed. Here, at the most northerly tip of Newfoundland, the remnants of the first settlement of Europeans in the New World were excavated in 1960. Today, St Anthony (pop. 2,250) is a popular starting point for iceberg tours. 📖 *Q7*

SIGHTSEEING

L'ANSE AUX MEADOWS ⭐ ☂

Eric the Red from Greenland and his men came here in 1000 CE. The *National Historic Site (daily in summer 9am–6pm | admission C$12 | Hwy 436 | ⏱ 2 hrs)* has reconstructed earth huts, and there are exhibitions *(visitor centre)* illustrating the harsh life of the Norsemen.

GRENFELL MISSION

Around 1900, British Dr Grenfell was the only doctor in the region, visiting the remote fishing villages of Labrador by boat. He founded the Grenfell Mission and this museum tells the story. *Daily 8am–5pm |*

Moose in Gros Morne National Park

GROS MORNE NATIONAL PARK

The 1,805-km² park is a UNESCO World Heritage Site as it preserves the geologically unique west coast of Newfoundland with its fjords and mesas.

The *Discovery Centre* in *Woody Point* explains the park's natural

admission C$10 | 4 Maraval Rd |
grenfell-properties.com

EATING & DRINKING

LIGHTKEEPERS RESTAURANT

Delicious food by the lighthouse with magnificent views of the ocean and icebergs. Specialities include fried cod tongues, fishcakes and moose. *Fishing Point Rd | tel. 709 4 54 49 00 | C$-$$*

SIDER TIP
Cod tongues anyone?

LABRADOR

Covering a mainland area of 300,000km², but with only 27,000 inhabitants, this part of the province is truly one of the last wild regions on earth. It is only since the recent completion of Highway 510 that a round trip on Labrador has become possible.

Take the ferry from the northern tip of Newfoundland to *Blanc Sablon,* then drive via *Cartwright* to *Goose Bay* where you connect to the Québec road network. On the north coast, a car ferry travels to the Inuit village of *Nain,* the springboard for tours to the *Torngat Mountains National Park.* 〰 M-Q 1-6

WHERE TO STAY IN NEWFOUNDLAND & LABRADOR

ART-HOTEL

What do you imagine a super-luxurious hotel at the end of the world would be like? Probably like the *Fogo Island Inn (Joe Batts Arm | tel. 709 6 58 34 44 | fogoislandinn. ca).* It's ultra-stylish, built and furnished by local craftsmen, with a fine-dining restaurant and a view that suggests the North Pole is within touching distance.

SIGHTSEEING

BATTLE HARBOUR ★

Bare rocks, colourful fishermen's houses and icebergs: the 250-year-old town, now a museum village, was once a cod-fishing centre. *Boat tours from Mary's Harbour | battleharbour. com*

RED BAY

On Labrador's south coast is a fishing village that was once the site of the first Basque whaling station – as demonstrated by archaeological excavations. The Basques sailed across the Atlantic around 1500, possibly even before Columbus (museum and visitor centre). It is now a UNESCO World Heritage Site.

DISCOVERY TOURS

Want to get under the skin of the region? Then our discovery tours provide the perfect guide. They include advice on which sights to visit, tips on where to stop for that perfect holiday snap, a choice of the best places to eat and drink and suggestions for fun activities.

① BOLD CLIFFS & SANDY BEACHES: THE ATLANTIC COAST

➤ Drive on the famous Cabot Trail high above the sea
➤ Ride a tidal wave on a raft
➤ Take a selfie at Peggy's Cove lighthouse

📍	Halifax	🏁	Halifax
↻	3,000km	🚗	13 days (42 hrs total driving time)
ⓘ	The best time to travel is June to August and early October. Some restaurants and B&Bs close for winter in early September, even though visitors come for the autumn colours.		

A blaze of colour on Highway 60

FAR-REACHING VIEWS FROM STEEP CLIFFS

Start in ❶ Halifax ➤ p. 104, *from where Hwy 7 winds eastwards along the flat south coast of Nova Scotia with its countless bays.* The long rows of white buoys in the dark water indicate that oysters are being farmed near the fishing villages. Small farms in the area try to grow vegetables in the barren ground. Some 150 years ago pioneer life must have been much more difficult – and lonely – along this coastline, as portrayed in the museum village ❷ Sherbrooke Village *(June–Oct daily 9.30am–5pm | admission C$16 | on Hwy 7 | sherbrookevillage.novascotia.ca).*

On the other side of the dam across the 1.5-km-wide and 65-m-deep Strait of Canso awaits a highlight of the trip: ❸ Cape Breton Island ➤ p. 109 with the national park of the same name. Starting from the old French fishing village of Chéticamp, the magnificent panoramic ⚑ Cabot Trail *leads around the park.* An ideal location to stay is ❹ Baddeck. Over the next three days you should plan some island explorations, such as a walk along the 10km Skyline Trail in the national park and a whale-watching tour from Chéticamp. Delicious ice cream, a local passion, is sold in small shops in the

DAYS 1–4

❶ **Halifax**

200km 2.5 hrs

❷ **Sherbrooke Village**

110km 1.5 hrs

❸ **Cape Breton Island**

80km 1 hr

❹ **Baddeck**

115km 1.5 hrs

town. Do not miss a day's visit to the beautifully restored Old French colonial town ⑤ **Forteresse de Louisbourg** ➤ p. 111 *on the south-east tip of Cape Breton.* Equally fascinating is the mining town of Glace Bay, *about an hour's drive north.* The ⑥ **Miners' Museum** *(daily in summer 10am–6pm | admission C$16 | 42 Birkley St)* shows how coal used to be mined in miles and miles of tunnels under the sea.

INSIDER TIP
Excursion under the sea

⑤ **Forteresse de Louisbourg**

55km 1 hr

⑥ **Miners' Museum**

DAYS 5-7

280km 3 hrs

⑦ **Pictou**

40km 1.5 hrs

IDYLLIC PRINCE EDWARD ISLAND

The way back from the island leads through lush green farmland *across the northern part of Nova Scotia on the Trans-Canada Highway. You will pass the old Scottish settlements of Antigonish, New Glasgow and* ⑦ **Pictou**, a busy harbour village of lobster fishermen whose work is explained in the **Northumberland Fisheries Museum** *(daily in summer 10am–6pm | admission C$8 | 71 Front St).* You will see mini lobsters, find out about their breeding and can adopt one. **Lobster Carnival** *is in mid July. The next goal is just a short ferry*

The Skyline Trail initially leads through forest, then along cliffs with fabulous views

ride away: the island province of ⑧ Prince Edward Island ➤ p. 112. It is famous for its wonderful sandy beaches such as Panmure Beach *on the east coast, just an hour's drive from the ferry terminal.* Then there is the tiny capital, ⑨ Charlottetown ➤ p. 113, that is definitely worth a visit. You should treat yourself to a two-day break: swim near the red sands of ⑩ Prince Edward Island National Park, take a bike ride along the coast and feast on lobster in fishing villages such as North Rustico. The island is small, so you can rent a room for three nights near the national park or the centre of Charlottetown, e.g. in the Hillhurst Inn *(8 rooms | 181 Fitzroy St | tel. 1 902 8 92 50 22 | C$$).*

THE WORLD'S GREATEST TIDAL RANGE & DINNER IN THE LIGHTHOUSE

The massive ⑪ Confederation Bridge *leads for 13km high above the waves of the Northumberland Strait back to the mainland – to Cape Tormentine in the very south of the Province of New Brunswick. Expansive marsh landscapes accompany the trip via Shediac to* ⑫ Moncton, *where you will find a rare natural phenomenon: due to a tidal range of 7.5m, the flow of the*

⑧ **Prince Edward Island**	
60km	40 mins
⑨ **Charlottetown**	
30km	30 mins
⑩ **Prince Edward Island National Park**	
DAYS 8–9	
70km	1 hr
⑪ **Confederation Bridge**	
100km	1 hr
⑫ **Moncton**	

Peggy's Cove lighthouse is a must for every traveller to Nova Scotia

Petitcodiac River reverses twice a day. You can often observe a 30–40-cm-high tidal bore when the salt water runs against the river. The hinterland is charming too: gentle hills, forests and farms accompany the *Trans-Canada Highway 2 to the provincial capital of*

⑬ Fredericton ➤ p. 115 with the nostalgic museum village of Kings Landing. Continue through the idyllic valley of the Saint John River on *Hwy 102 south to the* Bay of Fundy *and the historical commercial town of* ⑭ Saint John ➤ p. 117, where the tidal range in the harbour reverses the rapids in the stream.

You have to go further east *via Hwy 1 and Hwy 114 to* see the record-setting, up to 12-m tidal range in the ⑮ Fundy National Park ➤ p. 114. It's a great opportunity for a walk on the seabed, but be sure to keep a close eye on the tidal schedule. *Continue via Moncton to Trans-Canada Highway 2*. A nice detour beyond the tourist-beaten path is a *two-hour drive south-west of*

DISCOVERY TOURS

Sackville. The restaurant in the ⑯ Cape D'Or Lighthouse *(tel. 902 6 70 83 14 | capedor.ca)* offers great fish dishes with spectacular views across the Bay of Fundy. There are simple rooms in the guest house of the lighthouse if you wish to stay longer into the evening.

FRENCH FARMING VILLAGES & ENGLISH FISHING HARBOURS

Back in Nova Scotia, take Hwy 236 and Hwy 215 from Truro and you quickly reach the ⑰ Shubenacadie River for an unusual and very wet rafting experience. 🎯 You can ride the river's turbulent tidal wave for 18km upstream. Contact Tidal Bore Rafting Park & Cottages *(12215 Hwy 215 | Urbania | tel. 1 902 7 58 84 33 | raftingcanada.ca).* The route then follows the Fundy Coast *via Hwys 215, 101 and 1 westward into the* ⑱ Annapolis Valley. This valley, steeped in history, is where the first Frenchmen settled in Canada in 1604 at Port Royal. South of Annapolis Royal ➤ p. 108, *Hwy 8 leads through hilly woodland*. In the ⑲ Kejimkujik National Park ➤ p. 108 you will have the chance to experience "classic Canada": in a canoe on one of the placid lakes. On the *way back to Halifax along the south coast,* there will be more hustle and bustle in the picturesque harbour villages, such as ⑳ Lunenburg ➤ p. 107, Mahone Bay or ㉑ Peggy's Cove ➤ p. 107. Today, tourism is the main source of income for these villages, and you will find galleries and handicraft shops as well as excellent restaurants for a farewell dinner of fresh fish or lobster before returning to ➊ Halifax.

INSIDER TIP
Surf the tidal wave on a raft

---

⑯ Cape D'Or Lighthouse

DAYS 11–13
175km   2.5 hrs

⑰ Shubenacadie River

⑱ Annapolis Valley
85km   1 hr

⑲ Kejimkujik National Park
85km   1 hr

⑳ Lunenburg
100km   1.5 hrs

㉑ Peggy's Cove
75km   50 mins

➊ Halifax

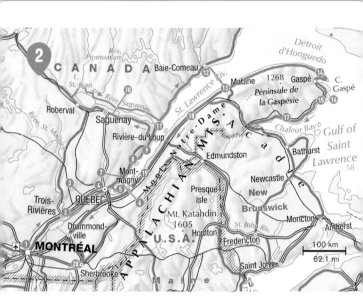

❷ ALONG THE ST LAWRENCE RIVER THROUGH NEW FRANCE

➤ Watch beluga whales in the fjord of Tadoussac
➤ Go on a pilgrimage in Ste-Anne-de-Beaupré
➤ Eat blueberry pie at Lac Saint-Jean

📍 Montréal   🏁 Montréal

🔄 2,900km   🚗 11 days (50 hrs total driving/ferry time

ℹ️ This route is nice in summer, but most impressive in early October.

DAYS 1–3

❶ Montréal

140km   1.5 hrs

❷ Trois-Rivières

ON THE BANKS OF THE GREAT RIVER

From the lively metropolis of ❶ Montréal ➤ p. 68, take *Hwy 40 through the fertile lowlands of the St Lawrence River* to the historic old town of ❷ Trois-Rivières ➤ p. 91. *Then follow Route 138 on the north bank of the* river that is now several hundred metres wide. The winding country road follows the old *Chemin du Roi*, which the governor of New France had built in 1737 to connect farming settlements with the large estates of wealthy landowners. You will see mansions, magnificent old churches and mills built in the Norman style in small places like ❸ Deschambault or Portneuf, reminiscent of the heyday of *Nouvelle France*. More history awaits in the listed historic centre of ❹ Québec City ➤ p. 85 and, just outside the city, the ❺ Île d'Orléans ➤ p. 91 with its nostalgic farming villages.

PILGRIMAGES & ZIPLINING

The next section also follows the north shore of the St Lawrence River: along the Côte de Beaupré ➤ p. 80 to the old pilgrimage destination of ❻ Beaupré and ❼ Parc du Mont Ste-Anne *(mont-sainte-anne.com | canyonsa.qc.ca)*. Here you can set your pulse racing on a fantastic, 60-m-high zipline. Or maybe you prefer paragliding or canyoning? *Continue on Route 138 to* ❽ Baie-Saint-Paul ➤ p. 95 where you can treat yourself to a night in the stylish hotel Le Germain Charlevoix *(145 rooms | tel. 1 418 2 40 41 20 | legermainhotels.com | C$$)*. It is part of an ecological project by the creative (and wealthy) founder of Cirque du Soleil. An afternoon in the hotel's luxurious spa is highly recommended. *The winding Route 362 on the high bank of the river offers great views and leads to the beautifully situated village of* ❾ La Malbaie, with its numerous art galleries. *Route 170 then takes you to the* mountains and the almost Norwegian-looking fjords of the ❿ Saguenay Region ➤ p. 96 and to lake Lac Saint-Jean. Old industrial places like Chicoutimi – a stronghold of Québec separatists – alternate with sleepy villages, rugged high banks and beaches on the lake. Don't leave without trying the local blueberry pie, available in Saint-Félicien at the Pâtisserie Chez Grand-Maman *(1883, Blvd du Jardin | C$)*.

WHALE WATCHING ON THE ST LAWRENCE

Keep your eyes peeled as you *continue along Routes 172 and 138,* because you can often observe belugas and other whales at the mouth of the river Saguenay

70km	50 mins
❸ **Deschambault**	
65km	50 mins
❹ **Québec City**	
15km	20 mins
❺ **Île d'Orléans**	
DAYS 4–5	
50km	40 mins
❻ **Beaupré**	
5km	10 mins
❼ **Parc du Mont Ste-Anne**	
60km	50 mins
❽ **Baie-Saint-Paul**	
50km	40 mins
❾ **La Malbaie**	
175km	2 hrs
❿ **Saguenay-Region**	
DAY 6	
150km	1.5 hrs

⑪ Tadoussac	
200km	1.5 hrs
⑫ Baie-Comeau	

DAYS 7-9

70km	2.5 hrs
⑬ Gaspésie	
300 km	3.5 hrs
⑭ Parc national de Forillon	
120km	1.5 hrs
⑮ Percé	
4km	20 mins
⑯ Île Bonaventure	
125km	1.5 hrs
⑰ Baie des Chaleurs	

DAYS 10-11

450km	5 hrs
⑱ Parc national du Bic	
175km	2 hrs
⑲ St-Jean-Port-Joli	
350km	3.5 hrs
⑳ Eastern Townships	
150km	2 hrs

① Montréal

and on the St Lawrence. An even better experience is to take a two- to three-hour boat ride from ⑪ Tadoussac, e.g. with Otis Excursion *(431, Bateau-Passeur | tel. 1 418 2 35 41 97 | otisexcursions.com)*. On the route to ⑫ Baie-Comeau ➤ p. 98 you will get great views across the St Lawrence River. The mountains huddle closer to the coast, the landscape becomes more remote and acquires a harsh Nordic touch.

The journey by car ferry leads to the south bank of the St Lawrence River that looks almost like a bay now. From the destination port of Matane, Route 132 follows the coast around the densely forested peninsula of ⑬ Gaspésie ➤ p. 92. *The scenic route reaches its dramatic climax in the* ⑭ Parc national de Forillon. The simple 8-km hike along Les Graves is quite beautiful: pebble beaches

INSIDER TIP
Cliff hiking above the se

alternate with steep cliffs and bizarre rock formations on the way to the lighthouse of Cap Gaspé. You should stay for a day at the village of ⑮ Percé: fwhere you can take a walk on the beach and a boat trip to the bird colonies of the ⑯ Île Bonaventure ➤ p. 94. Sunny resorts on the ⑰ Baie des Chaleurs line the distant route around the peninsula.

FOREST, LAKES & PRETTY VILLAGES

Stay on Route 132 as you head back west to the St Lawrence River valley. Interesting along the way are the ⑱ Parc national du Bic near Rimouski and the wood-carving village of ⑲ St-Jean-Port-Joli. You should *detour from the highway on Route 20 on your return from Québec City to Montréal and then take Route 55 south towards* Magog ➤ p. 91 *and the farmland of the* ⑳ Eastern Townships. This region, originally populated by the British, has forest-encircled lakes and small idyllic villages such as North Hatley, and makes a great detour for an agreeable end to this fascinating journey before you *take Route 10 back to* ① Montréal.

Whale-watching tours are highly popular, although sometimes you may only see dolphins

❸ ONTARIO: INTO THE LAND OF THE IROQUOIS & OJIBWA

➤ Canoe on remote lakes in Algonquin Park
➤ Be a spectator at a First Nations pow-wow
➤ Buy sausages from German Mennonites in Kitchener

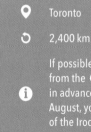

📍 Toronto   🏁 Toronto

🔄 2,400 km   🚗 14 days (32 hrs total driving/ferry time)

ℹ️ If possible, book the ferry *MS Chi-Cheemaun* from the ❿ **Bruce Peninsula** to ⓫ **Manitoulin Island** in advance: tel. 800 2 65 31 63. If you travel in July/ August, you can experience the pow-wow celebrations of the Iroquois.

URBAN FLAIR & FALLING WATERS

1 Toronto ➤ p. 38 deserves a day or two for a visit to the CN Tower, a stroll through the city, an afternoon's shopping in the Eaton Centre and – for shoe lovers – a visit to the Bata Shoe Museum. You only have to travel *130km on the Queen Elizabeth Way (Hwy 403)* before you reach Ontario's most famous attraction: **2 Niagara Falls** ➤ p. 54. From there you continue on side roads. *First, follow the Niagara Parkway to the historic town of* **3 Niagara-on-the-Lake** ➤ p. 56 where there are wineries such as **Peller Estates Winery** *(tasting and gourmet restaurant; daily in summer Sun–Thu 10am–9pm, Fri/Sat 10am–10pm | 290 John St E | peller. com). The route leads through the orchards of St Catharines into the land of the Iroquois and the* **4 Six Nations Reserve** *near Ohsweken,* where pow-wows are held at the end of July and the end of August. You can buy moccasins and First Nation art at **Iroqrafts** *(1880 Tuscarora Rd. | iroqrafts.com)* Next door, in **5 Brantford**, the excellent museum of the **Woodland Cultural Centre** *(Mon–Fri 9am–4pm, Sat 10am–5pm | admission C$7 | 184 Mohawk St | woodlandcultural centre.ca)* illustrates the history of Canada from the

A vineyard makes a rewarding stop on the route to Niagara-on-the-Lake

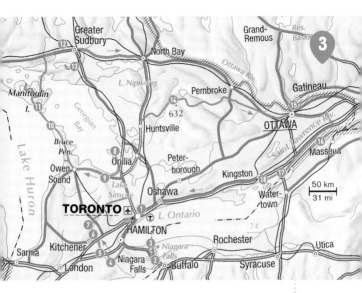

perspective of the First Nations. *Continue on Hwy 24 and Hwy 8 to* ⑥ Kitchener ➤ p. 56, the old city of the Germans in Canada. The farmland around the city is mainly settled by Mennonites who sell their own products, including the famous sausages, at the large farmer's market in ⑦ St Jacobs.

Continue your journey on country roads via Elora to Hwy 400 and north to Georgian Bay at Lake Huron. ⑧ Midland ➤ p. 64 was once an important settlement centre of the Huron tribe. It is well worthwhile taking a boat trip to 30,000 Islands and a trip to the suburb of Penetanguishene, where the museum village Discovery Harbour shows the life of the white soldiers and settlers 200 years ago. Sunbathers might prefer ⑨ Wasaga Beach ➤ p. 64 and Collingwood Beach. *Then take Hwys 92, 26 and 6 westwards along Georgian Bay.* Now it's time to stop for a day on ⁂ *Sauble Beach* or at the tip of the ⑩ Bruce Peninsula in the national park of the same name. Here, in Tobermory, you will find quiet bays with crystal-clear water and trails along the rocky coastline. And for divers there are exciting wreck dives. Great for one night with a view of the sea is

⑥ **Kitchener**	
20km	20 mins
⑦ **St Jacobs**	
DAYS 4–6	
200km	2.5 hrs
⑧ **Midland**	
40km	40 mins
⑨ **Wasaga Beach**	
200km	2.5 hrs
⑩ **Bruce Peninsula**	
45km	1.5 hrs

the Grandview Motel *(8 rooms | 8 Earl St | tel. 1 519 5 96 22 20 | C$$)* in Tobermory.

BEACH LIFE & CANOEING

A short ferry ride on the 'MS Chi-Cheemaun' takes you north to ⑪ Manitoulin Island ➤ p. 65, the island of the Ojibwa First Nation. In the museum of the Ojibwe Cultural Foundation *(ojibweculture.ca)* in West Bay you will learn about the culture of the Ojibwa. On the Kicking Mule Ranch *(Hwy 6 | tel. 1 705 8 59 12 34 | manitoulin-island.com/kmr)* you can go riding in the woods – and dance festivals will be held on many weekends during the summer. *Hwy 6 leads north through a wild and romantic landscape to the mainland and then, through lonely forests on the Trans-Canada Highway, to the mining town of* ⑫ Sudbury ➤ p. 65. Wildlife fans can take a (multi-day) canoe trip in the largely untouched ⑬ Killarney Provincial Park south of the town (boat hire on Hwy 637).

Continue on the Trans-Canada Highway to North Bay on the shores of Lake Nipissing and then south to Huntsville. For a whole day the route runs through the typical landscape of the Canadian Shield – forests, lakes and granite rocks as far as the eye can see. The scenery is quite similar on Hwy 60 in the ⑭ Algonquin Provincial Park ➤ p. 63 where you have a good chance of seeing moose and beavers along the trails or on a canoe trip. This is how you imagine Canada! Park the car for a day, hire a canoe at Opeongo Lake, the largest lake in the Algonquin Park, and discover the wilderness. You can have the canoe transported into the hinterland by water taxi. Route advice, canoeing and camping gear are available directly at the lake from Opeongo Store & Water Taxi *(bookings tel. 1 613 6 37 20 75 | algonquin-outfitters.com).* For overnight trips you will find many beautiful campsites along the lakefront.

INSIDER TIP

Take a taxi t solitude

MUSEUM CITY OF OTTAWA & THOUSAND ISLANDS

In the broad valley of the Ottawa River things become more civilised once again: small farms, apple orchards and vegetable fields line *Hwy 17 to the federal capital,* ⑮ Ottawa ➤ p. 59. You should spend a day there as the city has excellent museums and beautiful promenades. *Follow Hwy 417 and Hwy 138 to Cornwall* into the St Lawrence River valley and, on the bank of the river, follow the idyllic *panoramic route of the Long Sault Parkway to* ⑯ Morrisburg ➤ p. 63 and the museum village of Upper Canada Village. The last part of the route runs *along the broad St Lawrence River through the scenic island world of* ⑰ Thousand Islands (boat trips from Gananoque) to the historic university city of ⑱ Kingston ➤ p. 58. Then *take Hwy 401 on the north shore of Lake Ontario back to* ① Toronto.

DAYS 11-14	
285km	3 hrs
⑮ Ottawa	
140km	1.5 hrs
⑯ Morrisburg	
100km	1 hr
⑰ Thousand Islands	
40km	40 mins
⑱ Kingston	
260km	3 hrs
① Toronto	

The view over the roof of Ottawa's Parliament building

GOOD TO KNOW

HOLIDAY BASICS

ARRIVAL

Time zones

Nova Scotia, Prince Edward Island and New Brunswick follow Atlantic Standard Time (4 hours behind the UK). Newfoundland is 3.5 hours behind the UK. Québec and most of Ontario are on Eastern Standard Time (5 hours behind the UK). Daylight Saving Time runs from the second Sunday in March to the first Sunday in November.

Air Canada and most national carriers have regular flights to Toronto and Montréal. The best option for flying to Newfoundland or Halifax is with *Air Canada* from London.

From Toronto Airport (YYZ) there are fast train connections, taxis and airport buses to the city centre. The major car rental companies such as *Avis*, *Hertz* and *Alamo/National* have representatives at all airports.

GETTING AROUND

BUS & TRAIN

Greyhound, *Megabus* and *Maritime Bus* connect all major towns.

The legendary coast-to-coast Toronto to Vancouver train is a great way to see Canada and must be booked a few months in advance. Other lines go from Montréal to the Gaspésie Peninsula and Halifax. *VIA Rail (viarail. ca)* offers a *Canrailpass* for their entire

Vintage cars in Kensington Market, Toronto

network, a *Corridorpass* for Québec and Ontario as well as other promotions and packages.

CAR HIRE

The minimum age to rent a car ranges from 21 to 25 years.

🐾 Book hire cars or camper vans through an agent several months in advance: this is usually cheaper and safer because taxes and insurance are included in the price. Motorhomes are often fully booked in peak season.

If you break down or have an accident, you should contact the hire company immediately. They will arrange for a repair or courtesy car.

DOMESTIC FLIGHTS

Air Canada and some regional airlines offer discounted rates for intra-Canadian routes booked online. It is cheaper to include any domestic flights in transatlantic tickets.

Electricity – adapter types A & B

Current is 110 volts, 60Hz. Mobile phones, tablets, shavers and hairdryers from other countries will need a transformer and a plug adaptor for Canada's two-pin sockets.

DRIVING

It is compulsory to wear seatbelts. You can drive with your national driving license for up to three months. The road network is good, but the north of the provinces has fewer roads.

On major roads the speed limits are 80kmh or 100kmh; in towns 50kmh; and on motorways 110kmh. Traffic regulations are standard but there are certain unusual features: at traffic lights you can turn right on red (although not in Montréal); on multi-lane roads you may overtake on the right, but school buses – when they have their hazard lights on – must never be passed, not even when approaching from the opposite direction. The legal blood alcohol limit is 0.08%.

FERRIES

The ferries that operate on the St Lawrence in Québec and to Prince Edward Island run hourly and you don't need to pre-book. However, you should pre-book car ferries from Sydney/Nova Scotia to Newfoundland and in summer from Tobermory to Manitoulin Island in Lake Huron: *marineatlantic.ca* and *ontarioferries. com*.

EMERGENCIES

CONSULATES & EMBASSIES
BRITISH HIGH COMMISSION
80 Elgin St | Ottawa | ON K1P 5K7| tel. 613 2 377 15 30 | ukincanada.fco. gov.uk

US EMBASSY
490 Sussex Dr. | Ottawa | ON K1N 1G8 | tel. 613 6 88 53 35 | ca.usembassy. gov

EMERGENCY SERVICES
911 or dial *0* for the operator.

HEALTH
Medical care in Canada is excellent but expensive. Make sure you have adequate insurance for travelling abroad.

AUSTRALIAN HIGH COMMISSION
*Suite 1301 | 50 O'Connor St | Ottawa | ON K1P 6L2 | tel. 613 2 36 08 41 | canada.embassy.gov.a*u

ESSENTIALS

ALCOHOL/CANNABIS
In most provinces the legal age for drinking alcohol is 19, but in Québec it's 18. Some supermarkets sell beer and wine, but spirits are only available in *liquor stores*. Similar age limits and restrictions apply to the private consumption of cannabis, which has been permitted in Canada since 2018. However, any other drugs continue to be strictly prohibited in Canada.

B&BS, HOLIDAY HOMES
Log cabins in the woods, B&Bs, city apartments and cosy country estates: there is a great choice of accommodation beyond regular hotels. B&Bs are easy to book at *airbnb.com* or *bbcanada.com*. For a good selection of holiday homes and apartments visit websites such as *cottagesincanada. com* or *vrbo.com*.

CAMPING & YOUTH HOSTELS
Canada's public campsites are beautiful. They are usually situated next to the water in national parks, have firepits, wooden benches, water pumps and simple outhouses and cost C$10–40 per night. Private, luxuriously equipped sites can be found on the outskirts of cities and outside the national parks (C$20–70). Camping

FESTIVALS & EVENTS
ALL YEAR ROUND

FEBRUARY

★ *Carnaval du Québec* (photo, Québec City): boat races on the partly frozen St Lawrence, *carnaval.qc.ca*

MAY

★ *Canadian Tulip Festival* (Ottawa), *tulipfestival.ca*

JUNE

Grand Prix du Canada (Montréal), *gpcanada.ca*

Pride Week (Toronto), *pridetoronto.com*

★ *Festival International de Jazz* (Montréal): more than 1,000 artists from all over the world, *montreal jazzfest.com*

JULY

Lobster Festival (Shediac), *shediac lobsterfestival.ca*

Elvis Festival (Collingwood), *colling woodfestival.com*

Bluesfest (Ottawa), *ottawabluesfest.ca*

Juste pour Rire (Montréal): comedy festival, *hahaha.com*

Festival d'Été (Québec City): French culture in North America, *feq.ca*

Caribana (Toronto): parade with a Caribbean feel, *caribanatoronto.com*

AUGUST

Veld Music Festival (Toronto), *veld musicfestival.com*

Wikwemikong Cultural Festival (Manitoulin Island): powwow dances of the Ojibwa, *wikwemikongheritage.org*

Festival Acadien (Caraquet): festival of the French-Canadians, *festivalacadien.ca*

Canadian National Exhibition (Toronto): a gigantic fair, *theex.com*

SEPTEMBER

International Film Festival (Toronto), *tiff.net*

Niagara Grape and Wine Festival (St Catharines), *niagarawinefestival.com*

OCTOBER

★ *Oktoberfest* (Kitchener): the biggest beer event in North America, *oktoberfest.ca*

Far-reaching views at Lake Huron

spaces in national parks can be pre-booked at *reservation.pc.gc.ca*. There aren't many youth hostels in Canada, but *hihostels.ca* and *hostelworld.com* can provide information on the ones there are.

CUSTOMS

It is prohibited to take plants and fresh foodstuffs into Canada. Each person is allowed 200 cigarettes, 50 cigars and 200g tobacco as well as 1.14l of spirits, 1.5l wine, plus gifts up to a value of C$60 per recipient.

Duty-free when returning to the UK is 4 litres spirits (over 22%), 200 cigarettes or 50 cigars or 250g tobacco and other goods worth up to £390.

IMMIGRATION

Tourists from the US, EU and most Commonwealth countries (UK, Australia and New Zealand) require a valid machine-readable passport and an *Electronic Travel Authorization (ETA)*, valid for five years and available for C$7 at *canada.ca/eta*.

Short trips to the US, for example to Detroit or the American side of the Niagara Falls, are possible without a visa. Please note that children need their own passport even if registered in their parent's passport.

INTERNET & WIFI

Canada has an excellent network. Hotels and motels often provide free internet access; only luxury hotels charge a fee for ultra-fast connections. ☛ Computers in the lobby are often available free of charge. With your own laptop or smart phone you can connect to WiFi (free or with a password from the staff) in many coffee shops.

MOBILE PHONES

Most tri- or quad-band European mobiles only function in cities and in the south of the provinces (sometimes subject to high roaming charges), while networks can be surprisingly patchy in the vast hinterland. Ask your mobile phone provider about special rates and add-on data options before travelling.

INSIDER TIP
Check your internet access

It's cheaper to use phone booths or *prepaid long-distance phone cards* than your mobile. Cards are available at *petrol stations* and in *grocery stores*. For a long stay it is worth getting a Canadian SIM card and using it with your (unlocked!) mobile.

HOW MUCH DOES IT COST?

Coffee	*£1.70–3* *for a pot of coffee*
Beer	*£3.50–5* *for a glass in a restaurant*
Lobster	*£17–28* *for a lobster and side dish*
Jeans	*£34–58* *for original Levi's or Wrangler's*
Tour	*£40–67* *for a half-day tour by raft or bicycle*
Petrol	*£0.70–0.75* *for 1l of unleaded*

MONEY & CREDIT CARDS

The local currency is the Canadian dollar (= 100 cents). Bank notes are available in 5, 10, 20, 50 and 100 dollars and coins in ¢1 *(penny)*, ¢5 *(nickel)*, ¢10 *(dime)*, ¢25 *(quarter)* as well as C$1 and C$2. For current exchanges rates visit *xe.com*.

You can exchange foreign currencies into dollars at airports and in major hotels (although the rate may be poor), but not in banks.

Divide your holiday funds into various payment methods: approx. C$100 cash for the arrival, a credit card for the majority of daily expenses (Visa or Mastercard is accepted everywhere – at petrol stations, in restaurants, etc.) and a debit card which you can use to draw cash from most ATMs at a favourable exchange rate. To be extra safe, take a few hundred dollars in traveller's cheques.

OPENING HOURS

Shops are usually open Monday–Saturday 9.30am–6pm, large shopping malls Monday–Saturday 10am–9pm and Sunday noon–5pm. Supermarkets are often open evenings and weekends. Many museums are closed on Mondays.

POST

Post offices are open Monday–Friday 9am–6pm and Saturday 8am–noon. Drugstores often have post offices as well. An airmail letter or postcard to Europe takes approx. five days from major cities and eight days from the hinterland. Postage for a postcard is C$2.50.

PUBLIC HOLIDAYS

1 Jan	New Year's Day/Jour de l'An
March/April	Good Friday, Easter Monday
Mon before 25 May	Victoria Day/ Jour de la Reine
24 June	Fête de la Saint-Jean-Baptiste (national holiday in Québec)
1 July	Canada Day / Fête du Canada
1st Mon in Aug	Provincial holiday (except for Québec and Newfoundland)
1st Mon in Sept	Labour Day / Fête du Travail
2nd Mon in Oct	Thanksgiving/ Action de Grâce
11 Nov	Remembrance Day/ Jour du Souvenir
25/26 Dec	Christmas/Noël

SMOKING

There is a smoking ban in all public buildings, at airports and in restaurants. Smoking is extremely expensive and is no longer regarded as acceptable.

TAX

Canada has a 5% *Goods and Services Tax (GST)* plus hotel taxes and regional duties. Taxes are only added to the purchase price at the cash register. In Ontario and the Atlantic provinces all taxes are combined into one *Harmonised Sales Tax (HST)* of 12%–15%.

TELEPHONE NUMBERS

All Canadian telephone numbers have ten digits: a three-digit *area code* plus a seven-digit number. For long-distance calls within Canada, dial an additional "1" before the area code. If you have problems phoning, talk to the *operator* (dial "0"). Toll-free numbers start with 800, 866, 877 or 888.

If you want to call a number in the UK, dial 01144, followed by the area code, omitting the initial "0". Then dial the actual number.

For calling a number in Canada from the UK, dial 001 plus the Canadian number.

Telephone booths have all but disappeared, with a few exceptions at airports, in malls and hotels. Local calls are charged between C$1–2, whereas the long-distance call fee is announced after you have dialled. Hotels may have high surcharges.

TIPPING

A service charge is not included in restaurants and the standard tip is 15–18%. Hotel porters get about C$1–2 per item of luggage.

TOURIST INFORMATION

The Canadian Tourist Office website *canada.travel* provides extensive information about Canada's attractions and activities, plus links to the individual provinces.

WHEN TO GO

Apart from the Atlantic coast and St Lawrence Valley, Eastern Canada has an extreme continental climate with cold winters and hot summers. Best travel times (and high season) are from mid-June to late August, but May and September are often just as pleasant – with sunny days and cool nights. In early October the vibrant autumnal colours produce a stunning display that is well worth seeing.

Rocher Percé, Gaspésie, Québec

WEATHER IN MONTRÉAL

High season
Low season

	JAN	FEB	MARCH	APRIL	MAY	JUNE	JULY	AUG	SEPT	OCT	NOV	DEC
Daytime temperatures	–5°	–5°	2°	10°	18°	23°	26°	25°	19°	13°	5°	–3°
Night-time temperatures	–13°	–13°	–6°	5°	8°	14°	17°	16°	11°	5°	–1°	–10°
☀	3	4	5	6	7	7	8	7	6	4	2	2
☂	10	11	7	8	10	9	10	10	7	10	12	12

☀ Hours of sunshine per day   ☂ Rainfall days per month

USEFUL PHRASES IN FRENCH

SMALLTALK

yes/no/perhaps	oui/non/peut être
please	s'il vous plaît
thank you	merci
Good morning!/evening!/night!	Bonjour!/Bonsoir!/Bonne nuit!
Hello!/Goodbye!	Salut!/Salut!/Au revoir!
My name is …	Je m'appelle …
I come from …	Je suis de …
Excusez me!	Pardon!
Sorry?	Comment?
I (don't) like this.	Ça (ne) me plaît (pas).
I would like …	Je voudrais …
Do you have…?	Avez-vous?

SYMBOLS

EATING & DRINKING

The menu please.	La carte, s'il vous plaît.
May I please have …?	Puis-je avoir … s'il vous plaît?
bottle/carafe/glass	bouteille/carafe/verre
knife/fork/spoon	couteau/fourchette/cuillère
salt/pepper/sugar	sel/poivre/sucre
vinegar/oil	vinaigre/huile
milk/cream/lemon	lait/crème/citron
with/without ice/carbonated	avec/sans glaçons/gaz
vegetarian	végétarien(ne)
Can I have the bill please?	Je voudrais payer, s'il vous plaît.

MISCELLANEOUS

Where is …?/Where are …?	Où est …?/Où sont …?
What time is it?	Quelle heure est-il?
today/tomorrow/yesterday	aujourd'hui/demain/hier
How much is …?	Combien coûte …?
Where can I get internet access/Wi-Fi?	Où puis-je trouver un accès à internet/wi-fi?
Help!/Careful!	Au secours!/Attention!
fever/pain	fièvre/douleurs
pharmacy/chemist	pharmacie/droguerie
open/closed	ouvert/fermé
good/bad	bon/mauvais
left/right/straight ahead	à gauche/à droite/tout droit
breakdown/garage	panne/garage
timetable/ticket	horaire/billet
0/1/2/3/4/5/6/7/8/9/10/100/1000	zéro/un, une/deux/trois/quatre/cinq/six/sept/huit/neuf/dix/cent/mille

HOLIDAY VIBES
FOR RELAXATION & CHILLING

FOR BOOKWORMS & FILM BUFFS

📖 SHADOWS ON THE ROCK

In her 2009 novel, Willa Cather documents the hard times faced by French colonialists in New France. Nuns and prostitutes, settlers, trappers and prisoners – all lovingly portrayed, but the story is also disturbing.

📖 THREE DAY ROAD

Author Joseph Boyden, himself of indigenous descent, tells the story of a young Cree who, returning from World War I, finds healing with the help of his aunt Niska.

🎥 TAKE THIS WALTZ

A 2013 film in which the Canadian indie director Sarah Polley depicts a love triangle in Toronto – highly poetic and not at all cheesy.

🎥 MAUDIE

In the 1930s, Maud Dowley grows up in a remote village in Nova Scotia. Despite severe arthritis and a hard life, she becomes a gifted naive painter. The film, which debuted in Europe in 2017, draws a moving portrait. She painted the inside of her small house, now on display in the Art Gallery of Nova Scotia in Halifax.

PLAYLIST

⟳ ◄ ❚❚ ►► ◄))

0:58

❚❚ **LEONARD COHEN** – SUZANNE
The first and biggest hit of the legendary singer songwriter from Montréal

▶ **NATALIE MACMASTER** – THE CHASE
Enthralling fiddle music by the best violinist in Atlantic Canada

▶ **ARCADE FIRE** – REFLEKTOR
The fifth album of Canada's most celebrated indie band

▶ **MY HEART WILL GO ON** – CELINE DION
Classic song by the Québec artist

▶ **SHANIA TWAIN** – YOU'RE STILL THE ONE
Country pop by Canada's famous country singer

▶ **AVRIL LAVIGNE** – HEAD ABOVE WATER
Hypnotic sounds by the megastar who made a comeback after a long break

The holiday soundtrack is available at **Spotify** under **MARCO POLO** Canada

Or scan the code with the Spotify app

ONLINE

@BLOGTO, @VOIR
News from Toronto and Montréal. Associated websites with information on nightlife, art, ice hockey and restaurants. Plus blogs and videos.

CORRIDORCANADA.CA
Everything about Francophile Canada: culture, attractions, events.

LIVE NATION
Ticket centre for concert tours of big stars as well as many clubs and venues in Vancouver and other big cities. iPhone and Android app and Facebook page.

MUCH.COM
Music videos and news about Canadian pop and rock stars by the country's leading music broadcaster.

PARKS CANADA NATIONAL APP
App for iPhone and Android with descriptions of individual nature reserves, hiking trails and YouTube videos. The website features special pages on animal migrations, geocaching, etc.

TRAVEL
PURSUIT
THE MARCO POLO HOLIDAY QUIZ

Have you worked out what makes Eastern Canada tick? Use this quiz to test your knowledge of the region's best-kept secrets and most famous facts. The answers are at the foot of the page, with further information on pages 18–23.

❶ What is Canada's national sport?
a) Ice hockey
b) Lacrosse, a First Nations ball game
c) Ice hockey and lacrosse

❷ How many Canadians speak French as their mother tongue?
a) 20%
b) 30%
c) 40%

❸ Where was Greenpeace founded?
a) United Kingdom
b) Canada
c) USA

❹ What is the Canadian Prime Minister's hobby?
a) Ice hockey
b) Salmon fishing in the wilderness
c) Boxing

❺ Where do Canadians prefer to buy their donuts?
a) From the ice hockey player Tim Horton
b) From the US chain Dunkin Donuts
c) From the Hudson's Bay Company shops

❻ How many provinces does Canada have?
a) Seven
b) Nine
c) Ten

❼ Who were the Group of Seven?
a) Landscape painters from Toronto around 1912
b) Canadian soldiers fighting for Great Britain in World War I
c) A punk band performing on the banks of the Seven River

❽ What do you use a Zamboni for?
a) To turn Italian noodles into small works of art
b) To resurface the ice in a hockey stadium
c) As bait when whale watching

❾ When did the Inuit settle in Canada?
a) Approximately 14,000 years ago, from Greenland
b) Approximately a thousand years ago, at the same time as the Vikings
c) Shortly before Columbus, around 1450, from Alaska

❿ When does the so-called "Indian Summer" start?
a) Early August with the pow-wow dances of the First Nations
b) Early September when students return to outdoor nature classes
c) Early October after the first night frost

INDEX

The Chateau Frontenac as seen from Umbrella Alley in the Lower Town area of Old Quebec

WE WANT TO HEAR FROM YOU!

Did you have a great holiday? Is there something on your mind? Whatever it is, let us know! Whether you want to praise the guide, alert us to errors or give us a personal tip – MARCO POLO would be pleased to hear from you. Please contact us by email

We do everything we can to provide the very latest information for your trip. Nevertheless, despite all of our authors' thorough research, errors can creep in. MARCO POLO does not accept any liability for this.

e-mail: sales@heartwoodpublishing.co.uk

PICTURE CREDITS
Cover photo: Lake in Québec (Lookphotos: G. Schwermer)
Photos: DuMont Bildarchiv: Widmann (73); huber-images: P. Canali (6/7, 38/39, 43, 48, 50/51, 57, 61, 75, 80/81, 94, 138, 142/143), M. Carassale (34/35), C. Irek (115), S. Kremer (31, 68/69, 84, 90, 96), R. Mirau (146), Schmid (26/27, 28, 88/89, 106/107), R. Schmid (14/15, 100/101, 110, 125); Laif: F. Blickle (141), Grive (76), Linkel (12/13), Raach (18, 78); Laif/hemis.fr (8, 137, 145); W. Bibikow (87); Laif/Polaris (45); mauritius images: W. Bibikow (11, 109, 112/113, 154/155); mauritius images/age (104); mauritius images/Alamy (20, 27, 32/33, 58, 116, 126, 128/129, 130, 132), K. Bedell (122/123), R. Hicker (118/119), H. Schwermer (2/3), R. Stennull (Klappe hinten), H. Suk (10), B. Yuanyue Bi (9); mauritius images/Alamy/All Canada Photos (Klappe vorne außen, Klappe vorne innen, 1); mauritius images/Alamy/Stockimo/iaarts (23); mauritius images/Firstlight: K. Gillespie (30/31); mauritius images/Imagebroker: T. Sbampato (65, 66); mauritius images/Masterfile RM: D. Benson (98/99), D. Wilson (156/157); mauritius images/SagaPhoto: P. Forget (24/25); mauritius images/SuperStock (92/93); mauritius images/View Pictures: N. Lehoux (47); mauritius images/Westend61: W. Perugini (55); K. Teuschl (159); T. P. Widmann (62); Shutterstock: StaceyL (22), sockagphoto (28), Paul McKinnon (31), Katherine Kalmback (34), Lucy (49), lastdjedai (66), Benoit Daoust (78), Barisev Roman (91), JHVEPhoto (117), Vlad G (148-149), Salvador Maniquiz (158)

4th Edition – fully revised and updated 2022
Worldwide Distribution: Heartwood Publishing Ltd, Bath, United Kingdom
www.heartwoodpublishing.co.uk

© MAIRDUMONT GmbH & Co. KG, Ostfildern
Author: Karl Teuschl
Editor: Marlis v. Hessert-Fraatz
Picture editor: Gabriele Forst
Cartography: © MAIRDUMONT, Ostfildern (pp. 36–37, 131, 134, 139, inner flap, outer flap, pull-out map); © MAIRDUMONT, Ostfildern, using data from OpenStreetMap, Licence CC-BY-SA 2.0 (pp. 40–41, 52–53, 60, 70–71, 82–83, 86, 102–103, 120–121).
Cover design and pull-out map cover design: bilekjaeger_Kreativagentur with Zukunftswerkstatt, Stuttgart
Page design: Langenstein Communication GmbH, Ludwigsburg

Heartwood Publishing credits:
Translated from the German by John Owen, John Sykes, Susan Jones and Suzanne Kirkbright
Editors: Felicity Laughton, Kate Michell, Sophie Blacksell Jones
Prepress: Summerlane Books, Bath
Printed in India

MARCO POLO AUTHOR
KARL TEUSCHL

Karl loves the rough coastline along the Atlantic and thinks Nova Scotia wine isn't bad at all – which almost makes him a Canadian. The author and filmmaker lives in Vancouver and is the North America correspondent for German travel magazine *GEO-Saison*. For more than 20 years, he has travelled extensively in Canada and North America. "I find the amazing mix of cultures in the cities just as exciting as the little-known parts of this vast land."

DOS & DON'TS

HOW TO AVOID SLIP-UPS & BLUNDERS

DO REMEMBER THE MOSQUITO REPELLENT

Do not go hiking in the Canadian bush without mosquito repellent – the mosquitoes will have a field day! A small bottle of Off, Muskol or Cutter will make all the difference and keep the little blighters away.

DON'T UNDERESTIMATE DISTANCES

Distances can be deceiving, especially in the vast north of the country where the width of a finger on the map can mean a long day trip on seemingly endless dirt roads.

DO DRIVE SLOWLY NEAR SCHOOLS

The traffic signs are clear: you are only allowed to drive at 30kmh near schools. Stick to the limit as the Mounties are strict about this law; drive at a snail's pace when close to schools. Also, keep a look out for school buses with hazard lights. You are not allowed to overtake them or even pass them from the opposite direction!

DON'T DRIVE UNDER THE INFLUENCE OF ALCOHOL

The blood alcohol limit is 0.08%. In the event of an accident the insurance company will not pay out if you are over the limit. The police have no tolerance for drink drivers and there are tough penalties.

DO WADE SAFELY ON COASTAL MUDFLATS

It is said you should never turn your back on the Atlantic. This is sound advice. Freak waves can occur at any time on rocky coasts. Take special care in the Bay of Fundy: with tidal ranges of up to 15m, the tide can rush in at speed – fatal for reckless waders on the coastal mudflats.